India's Covid-19 Vaccine Drive

Manohar Agnani
Mahesh Kumar Aggarwal
Narendra Kumar Arora
Editors

India's Covid-19 Vaccine Drive

Management of Over 2 Billion Doses

Springer

Editors
Manohar Agnani
Public Heath Expert
Bhopal, Madhya Pradesh, India

Mahesh Kumar Aggarwal
Formerly at Ministry of Health & Family Welfare, Government of India
New Delhi, India

Narendra Kumar Arora
The INCLEN Trust International
New Delhi, Delhi, India

ISBN 978-981-95-8137-5 ISBN 978-981-95-8138-2 (eBook)
https://doi.org/10.1007/978-981-95-8138-2

This Springer imprint is published by the registered company Springer Nature Singapore Pte Ltd.
The registered company address is: 152 Beach Road, #21-01/04 Gateway East, Singapore 189721, Singapore

Foreword

डॉ. विनोद कुमार पॉल
सदस्य
Dr. Vinod K. Paul
MEMBER

सत्यमेव जयते

भारत सरकार
नीति आयोग
संसद मार्ग, नई दिल्ली – 110001
Government of India
NATIONAL INSTITUTION FOR TRANSFORMING INDIA
NITI Aayog
Sansad Marg, New Delhi – 110001
Tele.: 23096809, 23096820
E-mail: vinodk.paul@gov.in

October 24, 2024

India's National Covid-19 Vaccination Programme was launched by Hon'ble Prime Minister of India on 16th January 2021, with the aim to stem the rising tide of covid pandemic, and to reduce vulnerability and risk of mortality.

Covid-19 Vaccination aimed to cover the whole country incorporating its well-known diversity and heterogeneity. It indeed was the world's largest vaccination program of a scale, reach and speed which was unimaginable.

Over two billion vaccine doses were administered across India in just over 18 months. While the scientific and technical guidance was provided by the expert bodies such as National Expert Group on Vaccine Administration for Covid-19 (NEGVAC), National Technical Advisory Group on Immunization (NTAGI) and the Empowered Group on Vaccine Administration for Covid-19, the implementation was strategized by the Immunization Division at the Ministry of Health and Family Welfare (MoHFW) and was pivotal in determining the "How" component of each aspect.

The introduction of Covid-19 vaccines charted a new policy trajectory for India, aiming to cater to the varied needs of its populace with speed and quality. It encountered exceptional challenges, surmounted by a series of unconventional ideas that transcended traditional bureaucratic methods.

India emerged as the only country to support the end-to-end operations of the entire vaccination programme using state-of-the-art technology known as Co-Win, a remarkable Digital Public Good.

The program made a comprehensive communication strategy that effectively addressed both vaccine hesitancy and vaccine eagerness with real-time dissemination of factual and complete information about adverse events in a transparent manner while addressing the concerns of the population at large promptly.

In the wake of the unprecedented crisis of the pandemic, the MoHFW set a paragon example on leading through collaborative efforts. This involved 19 line ministries at the national level and 23 departments at the sub-national level, with the active participation of States/UTs and the ground-level support from NGOs and CSOs across the nation highlighting a remarkable example of unified action in response to the pandemic.

The vaccination program was a key component of the country's fight against the pandemic; that was led at the highest political level with vision, and at the same time its implementation was monitored on real time basis for all its nuances and complexities at the MOHFW level.

The book is an invaluable narration of the policy decisions and processes adopted for delivering the vaccines to over one billion population during Covid-19 pandemic.

This book is a stellar narrative of the challenges faced and strategies adopted by India to successfully and equitably vaccinating over 90% of the target population with two doses of covid-19 vaccine in a span of nearly one and a half years.

I feel the book will be extremely useful for administrators, program managers and students of public health not only as preparedness for future pandemics but also for influencing the performance of diverse health programs operated and implemented by MOHFW and state health departments.

Contributors of this book who played an important role in vaccination drive, have provided its ringside view and they deserve to be congratulated for their unique contribution.

(Vinod Paul)

Preface

The authors, as part of the national-level Covid-19 vaccination team in the Ministry of Health & Family Welfare, New Delhi, keenly realized the need of documenting India's Covid-19 vaccination experience. Through this book, the authors have tried to examine widely held assumption that only Covid-19 vaccine development and production represented a significant challenge, while inoculation merely fulfilled societal expectations of the healthcare system. The book also highlights how India managed its vaccine rollout, including the invaluable contributions of frontline workers, who deserve greater recognition.

The book examines the transformation of India's vaccine supply chain, emphasizing the need for rapid adjustments in response to rapidly changing vaccination policy, along with strategic "triage" system that optimized vaccine distribution. Co-Win emerged as a vital tool, acting as the central data repository for vaccination. The campaign's multidimensional communication approach addressed vaccine hesitancy through grassroots outreach and a robust media strategy. It also explores the legal framework, highlighting how courts balanced individual autonomy under Article 21 with public health needs. It provides insights into how virtual platforms facilitated nationwide training and empowered individuals across regions. The book explains how a transparent Vaccine Safety Surveillance System ensured community trust by addressing safety concerns with scientific rigor. The vaccination efforts by Indian states and union territories showcased innovative practices, including creative awareness campaigns and accessible delivery methods.

The book serves as a valuable case study for policy planners, public health professionals, supply chain managers, vaccine safety experts, communication experts, public health academia, and people engaged in Covid-19 pandemic period studies. This will prove to be an essential guide and a toolkit by providing valuable insights for present and future public health challenges.

Bhopal, Madhya Pradesh, India — Manohar Agnani
New Delhi, India — Mahesh Kumar Aggarwal
New Delhi, India — Narendra Kumar Arora

Disclaimer

The purpose of this book is to share the experiences and contributions of some of those civil servants and subject experts, who were working in the Ministry of Health & Family Welfare, Government of India, and were part of the team responsible for planning and implementation of Covid-19 vaccination efforts in India.

The editors recognize that delivering a project at this scale requires a multitude of efforts from the public, private, and civil society sectors as well as resilient citizens. The outcome of what became the world's largest vaccination drive in a large country like India was not achieved in a vacuum but was a culmination of many long-term factors such as strong leadership at all levels of governance, collaboration of several government departments, existence of a viable ecosystem for these services to be delivered, and large-scale documentation of data. It acknowledges the invaluable contribution of leadership at all levels.

While the book contains snippets of individual narratives from people who were a part of this system, it does not intend to undermine the great work done at all other levels that may not be highlighted in the book, due to several limitations related to compiling and relating those efforts to the ones cited in the book.

The scope of this book is limited to highlight the vaccination process adopted for world's largest campaign, which does not mean that other aspects related to vaccine development and production and creating an ecosystem are not important. In fact, we acknowledge that in absence of such atmosphere, documenting this work was impossible.

The authors have tried to remain objective in their accounts, but given their involvement in the vaccination campaign, the possibility of subjectivity in some places cannot be entirely ruled out.

The purpose of this book, is to narrate the massive planning exercise involved in the entire campaign, which may be useful as a case study to those who are part of leadership and governance and those involved in research for academic purposes.

All the data and figures in the book have been quoted from official sources and to the best of the authors' knowledge, but we acknowledge that establishing the authenticity of the data is at the sole discretion of the government. We also agree that in case of any discrepancy, or as more data becomes available in the future, the data presented by the government will prevail over what is stated in the book.

Introduction to the Journey of National Covid-19 Vaccination Programme

We are delighted to document and present the journey of the world's largest Covid-19 vaccination programme in India for several reasons. India's Covid-19 vaccination campaign is a testament to the exceptional teamwork and collaborative spirit in the face of an extraordinary emergency and was largely possible due to the country's continual efforts to strengthen health systems. One of the most important reasons for undertaking this venture to document the journey is that there are many unexplored aspects related to vaccination campaign. The book aims to offer a unique perspective to the readers through the documentation of these untold aspects, directly by those who were at the helm of affairs.

It also becomes important to record the campaign to counter the simplistic notion that Covid-19 vaccine development and production represent a significant new advancement, while inoculation merely fulfils societal expectations of the healthcare system. Through this book, we examined how the Covid-19 vaccination process differed from existing vaccination programmes in the country at that time. We contemplated the various innovative solutions and the hard work put in by the team to ensure vaccine accessibility and public safety. Our endeavour of the struggles of frontline workers through case stories aims to recognize their valuable contributions, which warrant necessary attention. We have also reflected upon whether the entire mitigation process has left us adequately prepared to face similar challenges in the future.

While charting this challenging yet remarkable journey, we considered how this book will benefit the community at large. We firmly believe that the methods of planning, execution, and management of a project of this magnitude confront and present readers with logical and rational answers to thought-provoking questions that arise when dealing with such emergencies. It also offers a potential replicable model for future pandemics and other public health crises, thus highlighting the need for a structured and authentic details word of the campaign. We also contemplated the potential academic value of this work and believe that presenting this in the form of a book will serve as a classic case study for public health students and a valuable resource for related courses taught in colleges and universities. Ultimately, we believe that this book comprehensively captures various untold and unrecognized aspects and will serve as an engaging read and a reference document for the future.

Well before the launch of the world's largest vaccination drive, Dr Manohar Agnani was made Nodal Officer and entrusted with the overall responsibility in the capacity of Additional Secretary, Ministry of Health and Family Welfare, Govt. of India. Dr Agnani was ably supported by Dr M K Aggarwal, Dr Pradeep Haldar, Dr Veena Dhawan, and the team of CVAC.

The chapters contained in this book are authored by those who have first-hand experience of being involved in such a gigantic exercise, which fact alone speaks volumes about its value. The authors, were part of the Ministry of Health and Family Welfare, Government of India. Collaborative efforts involved consultations with various State Governments, Union Territories, supporting Ministries, NITI Aayog, National Health Systems Resource Centre, Empowered Planning and Monitoring Groups, civil society organizations, development partners, vaccine manufacturers, infrastructure suppliers for vaccine storage, syringe manufacturers, vaccine and syringe procurement agencies, and Covid-19 vaccine testing centres and government vaccine storage centres at the state, regional, and district levels. This list is not exhaustive; it only illustrates the diverse stakeholders involved in the vaccination programme. The effective collaboration between the stakeholders enabled the world's largest vaccination campaign, demonstrating the power of effective teamwork and evidence-based decision-making in the face of a global health crisis. We have attempted to archive this very achievement through the various chapters of the book.

We begin by discussing India's response in tackling one of the most complex challenges that arose amid the high demand for vaccines—the prioritization of beneficiaries. The approach adopted was rational and ethical, focusing on achieving public health goals of preventing and minimizing infection, disease, hospitalization, ICU admission, death, and transmission. We then discuss the development of the Co-WIN platform, a groundbreaking cloud-based IT solution, which played a pivotal role in India's Covid-19 vaccination drive. Linked to the existing electronic Vaccine Intelligence Network (eVIN) platform, Co-WIN enabled equitable and inclusive vaccination access to all citizens and contributed to efficient management and data-driven decision-making.

Further, we explore the power of communication underlying the success of the programme. The world's largest mass vaccination campaign necessitated a multidimensional approach to provide accurate information, counter misinformation arising due to the "infodemic", address both vaccine eagerness and hesitancy, and promote Covid-19-appropriate behaviour. By effectively leveraging a combination of media tools, the programme could build public trust, leading to the world's highest vaccine confidence rates, as recognized by international bodies. This multifaceted media strategy serves as a global case study, highlighting the importance of tailored approaches for diverse populations and the power of collaboration between government agencies and media entities, providing valuable lessons for future strategies.

We also discuss the pivotal role of the judicial realm in scrutinizing and reshaping the vaccination policy. The judiciary's review of the logic, constitutionality, and regulatory decisions surrounding the vaccine approval process, the safety and effectiveness of certain vaccines, and the phased vaccination plan enabled a just implementation of the programme and lent credibility to the processes. This harmony of governance and justice was attuned to the nation's needs, transcended challenges, and propelled India towards its vaccination pinnacle.

In this grand endeavour, the strength of the nation's health workforce also proved to be pivotal. The book attempts to dissect the meticulous planning, dynamic training methods, and innovative use of technology that empowered a broad spectrum of health providers, across geographical barriers, to tackle the pandemic. The success of the campaign stands as a testament to the power of a skilled, motivated, and well-trained health workforce in realizing a healthier and safer world for all.

Various steps taken to adequately manage the cold chain infrastructure and syringe availability were vital. We explore the strong foundation provided by the country's experience in running the Universal Immunization Programme (UIP) which was augmented for the Covid-19 vaccination campaign. Subsequently, it highlights the timely measures taken to navigate the syringe demand, the culmination of which led to the administration of over two billion Covid-19 vaccine doses within 2 years, exemplifying meticulous planning and adaptability. The case for having a robust, transparent, and responsive Vaccine Safety Surveillance System undertaken by strengthening the existing AEFI Surveillance System during the pandemic is well established.

During a period when the country was grappling with the disastrous effects of the pandemic, the case study on Universal Immunization Program demonstrates strength and resilience of the programme, which is evident from WUENIC report 2022, which indicates that India's UIP coverage has not only recovered from the impact of Covid-19 pandemic but has surpassed the coverage of each antigen above 2019 levels.

The vaccination campaign in India against Covid-19 bore witness to a spectrum of inventive practices and successful approaches undertaken by the States and Union Territories. We quote a few examples of how each region meticulously customized its approach to tackle specific challenges and effectively engage its distinct population. Although the examples serve only as a representative glimpse, they give the reader rich insights into the innovations needed for a hugely diverse population and the replicability of such innovations for future situations. In this way, the collective efforts and innovative spirit displayed during the world's largest Covid-19 vaccination campaign in India have left an enduring legacy with far-reaching implications for public health.

The People Behind the Programme

The entire vaccination programme was guided by the National Expert Group on Covid-19 Vaccine Administration (NEGVAC), formed on 7th August 2020 and led under the joint chairpersonship of Dr V. K. Paul, Member NITI Aayog, and Rajesh Bhushan, Union Secretary for Health and Family Welfare. This group consisted of various experts from cross-cutting fields to provide a holistic viewpoint on the overall programmatic direction. The experts included Harsh Vardhan Shringla—Foreign Secretary, Dr T. V. Somanathan—Secretary, Expenditure well supported by Sanjay Prasad, Additional Secretary in the ministry, Dr Renu Swarup—Secretary, Department of Biotechnology, Prof. Balram Bhargava—Secretary, Health Research and DG ICMR, Dr P. D. Vaghela, S. Aparna—Secretary, Pharmaceuticals, Ajay Prakash Sawhney—Secretary, Electronics and Information Technology, Prof. (Dr) Rajiv Garg—DGHS, Dr Randeep Guleria—Director AIIMS, New Delhi, Dr Samiran Panda—Director NARI, Dr Rakesh Aggarwal—Member NTAGI and Director JIPMER, Puducherry.

The group also included the Additional Chief Secretary/Principal Secretary, Health and Family Welfare of five States as a way of inclusive representation—Mohammed Suleman from Madhya Pradesh, Dr Pradeep Kumar Vyas from Maharashtra, Amit Mohan Prasad from Uttar Pradesh, Dr J. Radhakrishnan from Tamil Nadu, and Samir Kumar Sinha from Assam, who shared their perspectives on the on-ground implementation of the vaccination programme. With the rich knowledge background, the team looked after the logistics, financing, engagement with manufacturers and state governments as well as ethical issues of prioritizing the target groups. Through 31 intensive meetings, the expert group played a vital role in the programme's journey based on the following guiding principles that laid the foundation of the vaccination programme:

1. Vulnerable groups should be identified and prioritized for early vaccination.
2. Vaccination of "Anyone, Anywhere" should take place, i.e., without imposing domicile-related restrictions for getting the vaccine.
3. Vaccination must be universal, i.e., no person should be left behind.
4. The entire process of vaccination of individuals should be supported in real time with the use of technology.

The technical foundation of the programme was furthered by the lens of the Covid-19 Working Group (CWG) under the National Technical Advisory Group for Immunization (NTAGI). The 24th NTAGI-STSC in June 2020 recommended the constitution of the CWG to review the existing evidence on Covid-19 vaccines, monitor new developments, and provide guidance on the safety and efficacy of the vaccines, high-risk population groups, and vaccine technology suited for each population group. This working group was led by Professor N.K. Arora, a well-known Paediatrician, Public Health Expert, and Vaccinologist with over three decades of experience and had other distinguished Vaccine and Public Health Experts including Professor Rakesh Agarwal, Gagandeep Kang, Navin Khanna, J.P. Muliyl, Pramod Garg, and Priya Abrahm. CWG met 54 times during the pandemic to contribute to critical vaccine related policy and programme challenges.

The Empowered Group for Vaccine Administration for Covid-19 (EGVAC) was further constituted under the chairmanship of Ram Sewak Sharma, CEO of the National Health Authority, to guide the development and evolution of Co-WIN. At the Ministry of Health and Family Welfare, the development of Co-WIN was steered initially by Lav Aggarwal, Joint Secretary, and later by Vikas Sheel, Additional Secretary, MoHFW.

The responsibility for planning and implementation of Covid-19 vaccination was entrusted to the Immunization Division of MoHFW under the leadership of then Additional Secretary & Mission Director NHM, Vandana Gurnani. The Immunization Division was headed by Dr M K Aggarwal, Additional Commissioner In charge of Immunization and Dr Pradeep Haldar, Advisor, Immunization. Both are stalwarts in the field of immunization and have successfully led the strengthening of India's Universal Immunization Programme (UIP), thereby enhancing the reach of life-saving vaccines to every child and pregnant woman in the country, even in the remotest locations. They were supported by the dynamic Dr Veena Dhawan who later took the reins of the Immunization Division. The Ministry deputed two very efficient young officers from its public health cadre to support this team—Dr Ashish B Chakraborty, who managed the legal and regulatory affairs of the vaccination drive, and Dr Suhas Dhandore, who was instrumental in shaping the Co-WIN platform.

The existing team at the Immunization Division was already overwhelmed with ensuring the delivery of routine immunization services amidst the pandemic. Hence, the team was further strengthened by inducting young public health professionals who would implement the ideas and vision of the leadership with minimum turnaround time, like Dr Ashish Chauhan and Dr Yashika Negi from UNICEF, to name a few. Both had previous experience of working at the Immunization Division and understood the minute nuances of how the system functions.

WHO also nominated Dr Satish Donakutty and Dr Aarti who brought with them grassroots-level experience, whereas Dr Kapil Singh from WHO supported the international alliances such as COVAX, APVAX, and Gavi among others, that contributed towards mobilizing vaccine delivery support, vaccine procurement, and securing sufficient supplies for the population. The technical wing of the National Health Mission (National Health Systems Resource Centre) was always available with its technical expertise and deputed Dr Palak Badhwar and Dr Sridevi, who were budding talents capable of thinking outside the box and suggesting novel solutions to the day-to-day challenges.

Similarly, the Immunization Technical Support Unit (ITSU) of JSI built an entirely new team that would look after the Supply Chain and Logistics for Covid-19 vaccination. This was led by Raman Kumar and Sanjeev Das who were supported by Dr Ajitendra Kumar from UNDP and Subhajit Chakraborty from NHSRC.

Media plays a very crucial role in shaping people's perceptions, particularly during crisis management and in the resultant era of an "infodemic". The open, honest, and proactive relay of information regarding the vaccination was led by Manisha Verma, ADG at MoHFW, heading the Media and Communications portfolio.

The role of partner organizations was phenomenal in this entire drive and deserves mention. UNICEF, UNDP, WHO, and ITSU stood by the MoHFW in drafting the entire operational guidelines for Covid-19 vaccination.

The UNICEF team, comprising of Luigi D 'Aquino, Dr Rija Andriamihantanirina, Dr Bhrigu Kapuria, Dr Mainak Chatterjee, Siddhartha, Tamara Abu Sham, Alka Gupta, and Sonia Sarkar, supported the Immunization Supply Chain Strengthening and helped in devising a robust communication strategy to tackle with vaccine hesitancy and eagerness. Dr Ashish Chauhan and Dr Yashika Negi from UNICEF, joined later by Dr Bhupender Khanuja, were working round the clock with CVAC at the Immunization Division and managing operational challenges that were encountered almost on a daily basis. Management of supply chain for syringes was well supported by Mr Gagan Shrivastava of the Ministry of Health & Family Welfare and Mr Supriyo Sarangi from UNICEF. Cold chain related works like procurement monitoring, assessment of cold chain space for storage of vaccines and supplies etc. was supported by the team from NCCVMRC led by Professor Sanjay Gupta and NCCVMRC Coordinator Dr Snehil kumar Singh besides Mr Gagan Shrivastava from MoHFW.

The UNDP team, comprising Abhimanyu Saxena, Dr Akash Malik, and Dr Pankaj Somani, supported the development and deployment of the CoWIN platform and also in the management of the Covid-19 vaccine supply chain through the existing eVIN platform. They were tasked with not just the technology development but also with supporting the readiness of users in time for the vaccine roll-out.

The WHO team, comprising Dr Pankaj Bhatnagar, Dr Danish Ahmed, Dr Sachin Rewaria, and Dr Vineet Goyal, supported the operational planning, capacity building of human resources, and Adverse Event Following Immunization (AEFI) surveillance for the Covid-19 vaccine. Dr Satish and Dr Aarti who were supporting the CVAC team were later substituted by Dr Paresh Kantharia and Dr Mujeeb.

The ITSU team, led by Dr Pritu Dhalaria and supported by Dr G K Soni, Dr Rajashree, Dr Deepak Polpakara, and Dr Vikas Madan, aided the daily compilation of coverage reports and AEFI surveillance.

One anecdote worth mentioning is that almost all the members of this team were medical professionals who qualified for the first category of beneficiaries of Covid-19 vaccination as Health Care Workers. However, each one of them waited for their age-appropriate eligibility for vaccination as they all believed that, amid the shortage of supply of Covid-19 vaccines, they should forego their eligibility for vaccination to those Health Care Workers and Front Line Workers who are managing the patients of Covid-19 and are on the field round-the-clock. They took this decision despite having a case of Covid-19 within the team every week. This team was at the Ministry every day without a break for more than 5 months before and during the vaccination drive. They even stayed in quarantine at home during this time to protect their families from being infected by them.

In the beginning the general situation regarding Covid-19 appeared to be quite grim and many well-meaning personalities came out with their apprehensions as well as valuable suggestions. To quote one example, an eminent personality like Nandan Nilekani wrote two-part article in the *Hindu* newspaper published on August 31 and September 1, 2020, sharing his apprehensions and suggested a possible framework for vaccine implementation in India.

It is heartening that many of the apprehensions expressed by him have been belied. At the same time many of his suggestions proved to be useful and were incorporated in the vaccination programme itself. For example; "*To train and certify a few hundred thousand people on how to administer vaccine, At least 100,000 vaccination stations can be set up across the country over a year, At 50 vaccinations per day per station, India could do five million vaccinations per day, A critical requirement will be supply chain, including cold chain infrastructure; People should be able to go to any vaccination station in the country anytime to get a shot; They can also book a slot online; The certificate can be downloaded to the person's smartphone, printed or stored in the digital locker, A digital record of vaccination & a link to self-reported side effects could strengthen India's vaccine safety surveillance.*" The country witnessed that the "Team Health India", with its efforts exceeded all expectations. In fact, it trained over 900,000 healthcare workers and administered 10 million doses in a day on several occasions.

In the last para of his article as mentioned by Nandan Nilekani aptly captured the mood of the country and had a hand on its pulse and concluded with a hope "*all arms of the government and public sector, private sector and civil society need to participate as partners. If we can take this approach, we will set a global benchmark on how to get past the pandemic. A combined response, leveraging each other's strengths, is self-reliant (atmanirbhar) at its best.*" We are happy that the success of "Team Health India" is testimony to the fact that ATAM NIRBHAR BHARAT has proved its mettle in the field of public health.

With all the tirelessly concerted efforts and strategic interventions leading to the successful administration of more than 220 crore Covid-19 vaccine doses in a span of less than 2 years across the nation, India displayed its exemplary capability to achieve such high levels of vaccination coverage for a sustained period of time. Despite the huge diversity of geographies and populations, India has been able to demonstrate how a huge vaccination programme can be mounted at scale. India has scripted remarkable achievements, from delivering 100 crore vaccine doses in nearly 9 months to 200 crore doses within the next 9 months. This achievement is not a result of overnight activities but be attributed on the whole to the amalgamation of the adoption of timely strategized measures, dedicated and efficiently skilled human resources, use of cutting-edge technology, mechanism of periodic reviews, and, especially, "Jan Andolan" (people's participation).

The story of India's National Covid-19 Vaccination Programme is a story of timely strategic decisions and innovations—in policy and regulations, in logistics and supply chain management, in social mobilization, and in good governance. It has served as an example to the world to follow. The programme as a whole has brought about the unparalleled all round comprehensive success of India in the face of the biggest public health challenge, so far. It has provoked thoughts globally for ways to strengthen the health systems overall. It is a textbook example to guide future generations to face any such crisis and bring a public health revolution. The nation's efforts and innovative approaches that ultimately led to overcoming various challenges and ensuring vaccination for all echo Nelson Mandela's words, "It always seems impossible until it is done."

We are happy to share this book and dedicate this work to all those Healthcare and Frontline Workers who lost their lives during pandemic, in the service of the nation.

Bhopal, Madhya Pradesh, India — Manohar Agnani
New Delhi, India — Mahesh Kumar Aggarwal
New Delhi, India — Narendra Kumar Arora

Contents

About the Editors

Manohar Agnani is a public health professional and retired IAS officer with over 25 years of experience in health systems strengthening, public health policy and planning, and human resources for health. He holds a master's degree in International Health from the University of Copenhagen, Denmark. He is currently a visiting faculty member in public health at Azim Premji University, Bhopal, India. He served as the nodal officer for India's national Covid-19 vaccination programme, for which the national Covid-19 vaccination programme team, Ministry of Health and Family Welfare, Government of India, received the Prime Minister's Award for excellence in public administration. He has published several papers in national and international peer-reviewed journals and has authored multiple books.

Mahesh Kumar Aggarwal completed his MBBS from Maulana Azad Medical College, New Delhi, India, and his MD in community health administration from the National Institute of Health and Family Welfare, University of Delhi, New Delhi, India. He was the former additional commissioner in charge of the immunization and Covid-19 vaccination programme at the Ministry of Health and Family Welfare, Government of India. He is also an expert member on three committees constituted by the Ministry of Health and Family Welfare, Government of India, including the National AEFI Committee, the Standing Working Group on Vaccine-Preventable Diseases (SWG-VPD) Surveillance under the National Technical Advisory Group on Immunization (NTAGI), and the standing working group on immunization, vaccine research, and capacity building (SWG-IVCRB) under NTAGI. He has published several papers in peer-reviewed national and international journals.

Narendra Kumar Arora, MD, MMSc (Clinical Epidemiology) completed his MD in paediatrics from the All India Institute of Medical Sciences (AIIMS), New Delhi, India, and MMSc in clinical epidemiology and biostatistics from the University of Newcastle, Australia. He is member of numerous national policymaking, scientific, research, and academic committees constituted under the Ministry of Health and Family Welfare (MoHFW), Department of Biotechnology (DBT), Biotechnology Research Assistance Council (BIRAC), Department of Science and Technology (DST), Indian Council of Medical Research (ICMR), and University Grants Commission (UGC) for maternal and child health, vaccine R&D, and health systems in India. Currently, he is the chair of the Covid-19 working group of the National Technical Advisory Group on Immunization (NTAGI), India, and also chair of several vaccine, drug, and diagnostic development related task forces in India; he is a member of the WHO's Global Advisory Committee on Vaccine Safety (GACVS), and WHO's scientific and technical advisory group for maternal, new-born, child and adolescent health and nutrition (STAGE); and he has been co-chair of WHO-STAGE for Immunization. He has published several papers in peer-reviewed national and international journals.

Abbreviations

ABHA ID	Ayushyman Bharat Health Account Number
AD Syringes	Auto-Disable Syringes
ADR	Adverse Drug Reaction
AEFI	Adverse Event Following Immunization
AESI	Adverse Events of Special Interest
ANM	Auxiliary Nurse Midwife
APHO	Airport Health Organisation
ASHA	Accredited Social Health Activists
AYUSH	Ayurveda, Yoga & Naturopathy, Unani, Siddha, and Homeopathy
BDS	Bachelor of Dental Surgery
CAB	Covid Appropriate Behaviours
CBC	Central Bureau of Communication
CC Space	Cold Chain Space
CCE	Cold Chain Equipment
CCH	Cold Chain Handlers
CCPs	Cold Chain Points
CDL Kasauli	Central Drugs Laboratory, Kasauli
CDSCO	Central Drugs Standard Control Organisation
CGHS Dispensaries	Central Government Health Scheme Dispensaries
CIF	Case Investigation Form
CMSS	Central Medical Services Society
CRF	Case Reporting Form
CSCs	Common Service Centers
CSOs	Civil Society Organizations
CVAM	Covid Vaccination Amrit Mahotsav
CWG	Covid-19 Working Group
DBT	Department of Biotechnology
DCGI	Drug Controller General of India
DF	Deep Freezers
DIO	District Immunization Officer
DTF	District Task Force
EGVAC	Empowered Group for Vaccine Administration for Covid-19
EPI	Expanded Programme of Immunization

ESIC	Employees State Insurance Corporation
EUA	Emergency Use Authorization
eVIN	electronic Vaccine Intelligence Network
EVM	Effective Vaccine Management
FIC	Full Immunization Coverage
FLW	Field Level Worker
GAVI-HSS1	Global Alliance Vaccine and Immunization Health System Strengthening Support-1
GFR	General Financial Rules
GMSD	Government Medical Stores Depots
GNM	General Nursing and Midwifery
GoI	Government of India
HMIS	Health Management Information System
HR	Human Resource
IAP	Indian Academy of Pediatrics
ICDS	Integrated Child Development Scheme
ICMR	Indian Council of Medical Research
ICSR	Individual Case Safety Report
IEC	Information Education and Communication
ILR	Ice-Lined Refrigerators
IMA	Indian Medical Association
IMI	Intensified Mission Indradhanush
IPC	Indian Pharmacopoeia Commission
IPV	Inactivated Poliovirus Vaccine
ITSU	Immunization Technical Support Unit
JE	Japanese Encephalitis
MAS	Mahila Aarogya Samiiti
MBBS	Bachelor of Medicine and Bachelor of Surgery
MCV	Measles-Containing Vaccine
MEA	Ministry of External Affairs
MGVS	Maratha Gramin Vikas Sanstha
MHA	Ministry of Home Affairs
MHRA	Medical and Health Regulatory Authority
MoHFW	Ministry of Health and Family Welfare
NCC	National Cadet Corps
NCCMIS	National Cold Chain management and Information System
NCCRC	National Cold Chain Resource Centre
NCCVMRC	National Cold Chain & Vaccine Management Resource Center
NCDC	National Centre for Disease Control
NEG	National Empowered Group
NEGVAC	National Expert Group on Covid-19 Vaccine Administration
NGOs	Non-Governmental Organizations
NHA	National Health Authority
NHM	National Heath Mission

NIC	National Informatics Centre
NID	National Immunization Day
NIN Hyderabad	National institute of Nutrition, Hyderabad
NIV Pune	National Institute of Virology, Pune
NMRRC	National Media Rapid Response Cell
NSS	National Service Scheme
NTAGI	National Technical Advisory Group of Immunization
NUHM	National Urban Health Mission
NYKS	Nehru Yuva Kendra Sangathan
OPV	Oral Polio Vaccine
OTP	One Time Password
PAN Card	Permanent Account Number Card
PCIF	Preliminary Case Investigation Form
PCV	Pneumococcal Conjugate Vaccine
PIB	Press Information Bureau
PIL	Public Interest Litigations
PIN	Personal Identification Number
PRI	Panchayati Raj Institutions
PSU	Public Sector Undertaking
PSUR	Periodic Safety Update Report
PWI	People Without Identity Cards
QC	Quality Control
RI	Routine Immunization
RISE	Raid Immunization Skill Enhancement
RPF	Railway Protection Force
RT-PCR	Reverse Transcription-Polymerase Chan Reaction
RUP	Reuse Prevention
RVV	Rota Virus Vaccine
RWA	Resident Welfare Association
SAFE-VAC	Surveillance and Action for Events following Vaccination
SAGE	Strategic Advisory Group of Experts
SARS-CoV-2	Severe Acute Respiratory Syndrome Coronavirus 2
SBCC	Social and Behavioral Change Communication
SDD	Song and Drama Division
SHG	Self-Help Groups
SIM	Subscriber Identity Module
SNID	Sub-national immunization Day
TCIF	Truckers Corporation of India Foundation
ToTs	Training of Trainers
TRIFED	Tribal Cooperative Marketing Development Federation
TTS	Thrombosis with Thrombocytopenia Syndrome
UHSND	Urban Health Sanitation and Nutrition Day
UIP	Universal Immunization Programme
UNDP	United Nation's Development Project
UNICEF	United Nations Chidren's Fund

UT	Union Territory
VAED	Vaccine-Associated Enhanced Disease
VC	Video Conference
VCCM	Vaccine and Cold Chain Manager
VHND	Village Health Nutrition Day
VPD	Vaccine Preventable Disease
WHO	World Health Organization
WHO-PQS	World Health Organization-Prequalification of Vaccines and Medicines
WIC	Walk-in-Coolers
WIF	Walk-in-Freezers
YRGCARE	Y R Gaitonde Centre for AIDS Research and Education
ZD Children	Zero Dose Children

The Universal Immunization Programme: Sustained Efforts During Pandemic

1

Mahesh Kumar Aggarwal, Kapil Singh, and Disha Agarwal

Abstract

India implements the largest Universal Immunization Program (UIP) in the world targeting 26.7 million newborns and 30 million pregnant women each year with 11 vaccines against 12 vaccine preventable diseases provided free of cost. India has made steadily progressed in childhood vaccination with Full Immunization Coverage (FIC) showing improvement from 62% in NFHS 4 (2015–2016) to 76.4% in NFHS 5 (2019–2021). However, it suffered setbacks during the Covid-19 pandemic due to multifarious reasons including diversion of health care resources to Covid-19 mitigation activities, the containment measures to prevent the transmission, and closure of Anganwadi centres, etc., and apprehension of the caregivers to bring their children for vaccination. The children who did not receive DPT containing vaccine (ZD children) increased from 1.4 to 3 million between 2019 and 2020 and as per HMIS.

To mitigate the declining coverage, the country declared immunization as an essential service and disseminated guidelines enabling the states to deliver routine immunization services during and pandemic. The guidelines were aligned with the containment strategy wherein containment zone, buffer zone and areas beyond buffer zone were identified. The outreach sessions were discontinued in containment and buffer zones while allowed in areas beyond containment and buffer zone. The guidelines to prevent transmission were adhered to while holding the outreach sessions. During pandemic period, the country organized

M. K. Aggarwal (✉)
Formerly at Ministry of Health & Family Welfare, Government of India, New Delhi, India

K. Singh
UNICEF, New Delhi, India

D. Agarwal
Former Senior Consultant – Immunization Division, New Delhi, India

M. Agnani et al. (eds.), *India's Covid-19 Vaccine Drive*,
https://doi.org/10.1007/978-981-95-8138-2_1

National Immunization Day for Polio Program and carried out regular Intensified Mission Indradhanush (IMI) every year from 2021 to 2023.

The efforts made to mitigate the impact of Covid-19 pandemic resulted in the recovery of the UIP as WUENIC report 2022 indicates that India's coverage under UIP not only recovered but exceeded that in 2019 during pre-pandemic period.

Keywords

UIP · Vaccine preventable disease · FIC · ZD children · Containment zone · Buffer zone · Outreach session · Intensified Mission Indradhanush · Covid-19 pandemic · WUENIC report · HMIS

India's Universal Immunization Programme (UIP) is the world's largest public health initiatives, aimed at reaching nearly 26.7 million newborns and 29 million pregnant women each year. The UIP provides vaccination against 12 preventable diseases, all delivered free of cost through approximately 13.6 million routine immunization (RI) sessions each year. The introduction of newer vaccines such as Pentavalent, Rotavirus, Pneumococcal Conjugate, Inactivated Polio, Tetanus-diphtheria, adult JE, and Measles Rubella has broadened the breadth of the protection.

Further, the catch-up vaccination campaigns like Mission Indradhanush and Intensified Mission Indradhanush are strategies which are periodically adopted for intensification of routine immunization, with a focus on the partially vaccinated and unvaccinated children and pregnant women, who have been missed through routine immunization. Similarly, supplementary immunization activities like Polio-National Immunization Day (NID) and Sub-national immunization Day (SNID) are being conducted since 1995 to bridge the immunity gaps for poliovirus in the community, which have contributed to eradication of wild polio virus from the country and getting certification of polio free status for India. With such strengthened immunization service delivery, the country's health system is aligning itself to the global goals of controlling and eliminating vaccine-preventable diseases (VPDs) and reducing preventable child deaths.

Government of India, over the years, has invested in UIP's key components such as capacity building of health care professionals and community health workers, bringing innovative training methodologies, enhancing cold chain capacities, real-time digital stock management, temperature monitoring, effective vaccine management and logistic supply, distribution mechanisms from suppliers to the cold chain points, communication strategies, supportive supervision, and structured review platforms from national, state, district to block level. Furthermore, well-established system for Adverse Events Following Immunization (AEFI) management and surveillance adds an extra layer of safety and efficiency to the program.

There is a structured program review framework of UIP, encompassing the State Steering Committee, State Task Force, District Task Force, and Block Task Force across all 36 states and Union Territories (UTs). The composition, standard operating procedures, mechanism, and meeting frequency are predetermined for these review platforms. Immunization-related data is collated in real time and analysed to provide guidance for corrective actions.

Recognizing the substantial human resources involved, the program conducts regular and refresher training sessions, which follow a cascade model, where key training sessions are organized with the assistance of technical experts and immunization partners. Further the vaccination team of AAA-ASHA, Anganwadi Worker & Auxiliary Nurse Midwife (ANM) are trained in the manner that they understand the power of advocacy and community engagement to build the trust and credibility among the community and bust any myth or misinformation related to vaccination.

Programme has a well-established mechanism for intersectoral coordination and has been getting support from various ministries, departments, professional bodies, associations, development partners and donors for routine immunization and campaigns.

An essential component of any vaccination program is the efficiency of its cold chain system, which is crucial for maintaining the effectiveness of vaccines. The Universal Immunization Programme (UIP) has notably advanced this aspect by establishing an extensive network of around 30,000 cold chain points across the nation. The success of which can be attributed to the innovative evidence-based programmatic and policy decisions achieved through institutionalized mechanism of National Cold Chain and Vaccine Management Resource Center (NCCVMRC), which was conceived in 2011 as a premier resource centre for the immunization division under the Ministry of Health and Family Welfare, Government of India. Beyond the imperative of maintaining a reliable cold chain system, UIP has undergone a transformative shift in vaccine and logistic supply management through the Electronic Vaccine Intelligence Network (eVIN). This smartphone and cloud technology-based application provides real-time insights into vaccine stock positions and storage temperatures at every cold chain point.

Country's Universal Immunization Program also stands out for having one of the most extensive Adverse Events Following Immunization (AEFI) surveillance programs. Further, the AEFI Reporting system under UIP is done on Surveillance and Action for Events following Vaccination (SAFE-VAC), a digital platform designed specifically for reporting serious/severe AEFI cases following immunization.

According to the findings from NFHS-5 (2019–2021), India has made significant progress in child immunization indicators, with more than three-fourths (76.4%) of children aged 12–23 months fully immunized, as compared to 62% in NFHS-4 (2015–2016). Similarly increase in the antigen-wise coverage is also noted between two surveys.

Vaccination against diphtheria, pertussis, and tetanus (DPT) serves as a global indicator for assessing immunization coverage and the effectiveness of immunization services. DPT-1 coverage specifically indicates the number of children who have not received the first dose of the DPT vaccine (Pentavalent) by the age of one, known as zero-dose (ZD) children. These ZD children are part of communities that have been missed by immunization efforts. They often experience various challenges, including socio-economic disparities, limited access to healthcare, and gender-related barriers, which can further compound their vulnerability.

UIP of India has been targeting un-immunized (ZD Children) and under-immunized children through routine immunization and catch-up drives viz. MI and IMI because of which the DPT-1 coverage reached the maximum coverage of 94% in 2019 (2019 WUENIC report). Similarly, DPT-3 coverage crossed 90% for the first time in 2019. MCV-1 also increased to 95% in 2019.

Improved immunization coverage has significantly contributed to decline in the mortality and morbidity due to the Vaccine Preventable Diseases (VPDs), which has contributed to the reduction in Under-5 mortality rate in India to 35/1000 live births in 2019 (Data source: Sample Registration System). Details are placed at Annexure.

This phenomenal achievement of UIP can be attributed to highest political commitment, domestic and external funding support, technical assistance from immunization partners and innovations such as electronic vaccine intelligence network (eVIN). However, the global healthcare systems faced significant challenges during the Covid-19 pandemic, causing severe disruptions to essential health services, including the delivery of routine immunization. The reduction in immunization coverage was primarily attributed to the diversion of healthcare resources to Covid-19 mitigation activities. Many states deployed human resources, including district immunization officers, block medical officers, PHC medical officers, and frontline workers, for Covid-19 duties such as managing quarantine centres and conducting surveillance. The simultaneous engagement of Auxiliary Nurse Midwives (ANM) and frontline workers in both Covid-19 containment and vaccination efforts resulted in a critical shortage of healthcare workers.

The containment measures hindered outreach sessions, leading to a decline in immunization coverage. Closure of Anganwadi centres, which are usually the main sites of outreach immunization sessions, and schools compelled the organization of routine immunization sessions at alternative sites, affecting service uptake. Similarly, the mass migration of the population to their native places during the pandemic disrupted the continuity of healthcare services, especially immunization. The community was apprehensive in coming to the health facilities and bringing their children for immunization due to the fear of contracting the disease.

As per WUENIC reports (2020 and 2021), globally an estimated 22.3 million children in 2020 and 24.5 million children in 2021 under the age of 1 year were left unvaccinated with basic vaccines. An estimated 16.1 million and 18.1 million zero dose (ZD) children, respectively, did not receive even their first dose of DTP containing vaccine. About 62% of these missed ZD children were in ten countries, including India.

Between 2019 and 2020, the number of ZD children increased from 1.4 to 3 million and the number of under vaccinated children increased from 2.1 to 3.4 million. MCV coverage also suffered with 6-percentage points decline from 2019 level of 95%.

As per HMIS, which is the Health Management Information System of India, the number of vaccination sessions that could be held, especially the outreach sessions, decreased significantly due to various challenges during the Covid-19 pandemic. Responding to the situation, the MoHFW, Government of India, issued guidelines in April 2020, declaring immunization as an essential health service and instructed the states to resume routine immunization. Health services including immunization were deemed as essential as per Ministry of Home Affairs (MHA) order dated 15 April 2020. Accordingly, MoHFW developed and disseminated guidelines for delivering immunization services during and post Covid-19 pandemic. Accordingly, special efforts were made to maintain routine immunization services, including conducting sub-national immunization days for polio and enhancing surveillance for Vaccine Preventable Diseases (VPDs). These guidelines were in alignment with the Covid-19 Containment strategy of the country, wherein containment and buffer zones were identified based on Covid-19 cases, as seen in Fig. 1.1. Areas where Covid-19 cases were reported along with surrounding areas with risk of Covid-19 spread were classified as 'Containment Zone' and 'Buffer Zone', respectively while area outside the buffer zone was identified as 'Area beyond Buffer Zone'.

Table 1.1 describes the Routine Immunization activities in different zones of Covid-19 containment. Birth dose vaccination continued at all health facilities, irrespective of the zone. In the zones of containment and buffer, outreach immunization services were discontinued (till the time the zone was categorized as containment zone), and immunization services at fixed health facilities were provided on demand

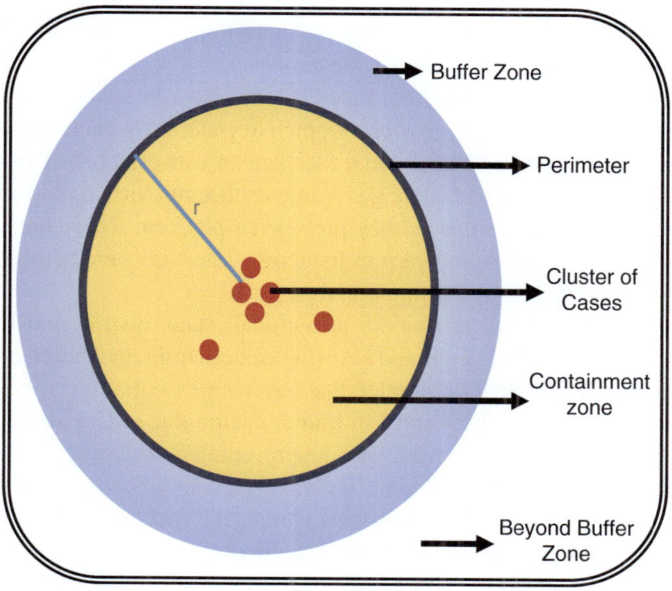

Fig. 1.1 Zones for Covid-19 containment. (Source: Guidelines for the containment of Covid-19 epidemic in the country (https://covid19dashboard.mohfw.gov.in/pdf/3ImmunizationServicesduringCovid-19OutbreakSummary150520202.pdf))

Table 1.1 Routine immunization activities in different zones for Covid-19 containment

Categorization	Birth dose	Health facility based session	Outreach session
Containment and buffer zone	Continued	No[a]	No
Areas beyond buffer zone	Continued	Yes	Yes[b]

Source: Guidelines for the containment of Covid-19 epidemic in the country (https://covid19dashboard.mohfw.gov.in/pdf/3ImmunizationServicesduringCovid-19OutbreakSummary150520202.pdf)
[a]Immunization services only on demand to walk-in beneficiaries in facility
[b]Modified outreach (VHND and UHSND) in areas beyond buffer zone

to walk-in beneficiaries in facility. In areas beyond containment and buffer zones, health facility-based sessions and outreach sessions continued. The outreach sessions were modified to prevent overcrowding by adopting a staggered approach, wherein a limited number of beneficiaries were scheduled for vaccination at a given time. States/UTs were advised to identify alternative vaccination sites in case of limited space to ensure social or physical distancing. They were also encouraged to address inadequate provisions for handwashing with soap and water at vaccination sites. Adherence to social distancing and hand hygiene was suggested and emphasized.

The need to follow universal Covid-19 prevention principles was reiterated, and the beneficiaries with flu-like symptoms were discouraged to attend the vaccination session. ASHA and AWW were suggested to adhere to the precautions for beneficiary mobilization. Significant efforts were also undertaken to conduct sub-national immunization days for polio and enhance surveillance for Vaccine Preventable Diseases (VPDs) during the Covid-19 pandemic.

To be cognizant of the challenges faced by the states in continuing the RI services, concurrent monitoring tools were adopted to generate evidence on implementation of risk mitigation measures; and a mechanism was established for review of immunization programme with state governments through virtual platforms. These reviews were of immense value as they provided a platform for exchange of ideas and cross learning to understand various local measures that were being adopted by the states for restoring immunization services.

Since the administrative machinery at national, state, district and block were busy with the planning of sessions and ensuring smooth implementation of Covid-19 vaccination, it was repeatedly reiterated that the other essential services should not get affected and the gaps in coverage in immunization due to Covid-19 need to be addressed on urgent basis to prevent vaccine preventable diseases.

On the recommendation of National Technical Advisory Group on Immunization (NTAGI), in year 2017, the Pneumococcal Conjugate Vaccine (PCV) was initially introduced in five states. Following an assessment of the disease burden of pneumococcal disease in other states, a decision was made to roll out PCV across the entire country. However, before the vaccine could be rolled out in rest of the states, the world was facing the crisis of the Covid-19 pandemic. Despite facing challenges such as the ongoing Covid-19 pandemic, supply-side limitations, delayed vaccine shipments, and staff shortages, India managed to successfully roll out the Pneumococcal Conjugate Vaccine (PCV) to the entire country in a remarkably short span of around 7 months. PCV scale-up during pandemic became the Indian success story. This was possible because of the resilient service delivery system for immunization, strong leadership, domestic financing, political commitment, Indian make vaccine, and new partnerships that developed during the pandemic crisis.

A pressing urgency was emerged to reach and immunize the children who did not receive due vaccines. Responding to the situation, India initiated the Intensified Mission Indradhanush (IMI) 3.0 in early 2021 (February and March 2021). This initiative aimed to address immunity gaps in areas where routine immunization services got severely disrupted by the pandemic. IMI 3.0 drive was done in 250 districts across 29 states wherein 0.95 million children and 0.22 pregnant women vaccinated.

To continue the catch-up efforts in the country, Government of India decided for another catch-up round, IMI 4.0, in 2022 (February to April) in total 449 high priority districts and approximately 5.9 million children and 1.5 million pregnant women were covered with due vaccines. The government's IMI strategy has focused on high-risk regions and intensified efforts among vulnerable populations, including migrants. In 2023, India continued its commitment to immunize the biggest catch-up cohort up to the age of 5 years and launched IMI 5.0 in all the districts of the country. The implementation of Intensified Mission Indradhanush (IMI) 5.0 was not just a vaccination drive but a visionary pursuit aimed at eliminating highly contagious diseases like measles and rubella, leading towards a measles-free India. This initiative demonstrated India's proactive approach in addressing challenges and turning them into opportunities for growth.

Each year WHO and UNICEF jointly publish WUENIC report on the performance of country's immunization program. The latest World Immunization and Evaluation Report (WUENIC) 2020 is the first to provide global estimates on countries' immunization performance immediately after the Covid-19 pandemic. According to the report, immunization services reached an additional 4 million children globally in 2022 compared to 2021. In 2022, approximately 110 million children received the third dose of the Diphtheria, Pertussis, and Tetanus (DPT)-containing vaccine, compared to 106 million children in 2021. India notably contributed to a 40% increase in global immunization services during the same period. It is important to note that India represents 17.6% of the total worldwide cohort of surviving infants.

In 2022, estimated 1.6 million children were under vaccinated in India who could not receiving the third dose of the DPT-containing vaccine. This figure represents a significant decrease from the number of under-vaccinated children in 2021 and 2019, which was 3.4 million and 2 million, respectively. When compared to global trends, it is observed that, in 2022, there were 20.5 million under-vaccinated children, a decrease from 24.5 million in 2021 and an increase from 18.4 million in 2019 (pre-pandemic levels). The comparison of India's performance with global figures reveals that while the world is still grappling to achieve pre-pandemic levels of immunization coverage, India has not only reached these levels but has surpassed the pre-pandemic coverage levels.

Similarly, the number of zero-dose children in India, representing those who did not receive any dose of the DPT-containing vaccine in their first year, decreased significantly from 2.7 million in 2021 to 1.1 million in 2022. This figure even surpassed the pre-pandemic levels of 2019, which stood at 1.4 million. Recent estimates indicate that, excluding BCG, India has not only achieved pre-pandemic coverage levels for measles-containing vaccine (MCV-1) and rubella-containing vaccine (RCV-1) but has also exceeded the pre-pandemic (2019) levels for other vaccines, including DPT-1, DPT-3, Oral Polio Vaccine (OPV-3), Inactivated Polio Vaccine (IPV-1), MCV-2, Hepatitis B (Hep-B) birth dose, Rotavirus Vaccine (RVV-3), and Pneumococcal Conjugate Vaccine (PCV-3). In 2022, DPT-3 coverage notably increased to an impressive 93%, surpassing the pre-pandemic peak of 91% recorded in 2019. Overall, the number of zero-dose (1.1 million) and dropout (0.5 million) children decreased to 1.6 million in 2022, significantly lower than the 2.1 million reported in 2019.

It is also significant to narrate that, globally, pre-pandemic coverage levels were achieved only for Inactivated Polio Vaccine (IPV-1), Measles-Containing Vaccine second dose (MCV-2), Hepatitis B (Hep-B) birth dose, Rotavirus Vaccine last dose (RVV last dose), and Pneumococcal Conjugate Vaccine third dose (PCV-3). While global coverage for the first and third doses of the Diphtheria, Pertussis, and Tetanus vaccine (DPT-1 and DPT-3) increased in 2022 compared to 2021, it did not reach pre-pandemic levels.

To sum up, the WUENIC report 2022 indicates that India's UIP coverage has not only recovered from the impact of Covid-19 pandemic but has surpassed the coverage of each antigen above 2019 levels. This is a testament of UIP's strength to simultaneously scale up PCV and Covid-19 vaccine across the country during the challenging times and continue the routine immunization services to an extent possible and later on bounce back from the odds.

1.1 Conclusion

During a period when the country was grappling with the disastrous effects of the pandemic, it could not afford to lower its guard against vaccine-preventable diseases. Lowering defences at such a time would have translated into the double calamity of the Covid-19 pandemic and an outbreak of vaccine-preventable diseases.

In such a critical time, the Universal Immunization Program demonstrated strength and resilience, and the response shown by the programme during the Covid-19 pandemic is an outcome of years of effort and investment. Furthermore, the robust framework of the UIP played a pivotal role in efficiently launching the world's largest Covid-19 Vaccination drives in a timely manner.

What is even more commendable is that the evolution of the UIP is ongoing. Building on the successes of eVIN and CoWIN, the UIP is initiating one of its most ambitious projects, the development of the Electronic Immunization Registry—U-WIN. The UIP strives to evolve and advance, with the single objective that no child should die of vaccine preventable diseases.

Role of National Technical Advisory Group of Immunization (NTAGI) in Covid-19 Vaccination Program

2

Narendra Kumar Arora, Awnish Kumar Singh, Dinesh Kumar, Kushagr Duggal, Renu Shrivas, and Krittika Bhaattacharyya

Abstract

The Covid-19 pandemic posed unprecedented scientific, programmatic and governance challenges globally; timely decision making was the key to guide public health action. The National Technical Advisory Group on Immunization (NTAGI), as the apex body for immunization policy in India, played a crucial role in shaping the country's Covid-19 vaccination strategy. To address the rapidly evolving situation, dedicated Covid-19 Working Group (CWG) was constituted in July 2020 to review evidence and program data and provide recommendations on surveillance, developing epidemiology, disease severity, vaccine research and development, real world vaccine effectiveness, vaccine safety and hesitancy and program preparation for vaccine rollout and associated logistics. Vaccine manufacturers shared pre-clinical and clinical data with CWG as an additional step to review the vaccine efficacy and safety beyond the usual regulatory pathway. The CWG met 53 times, held frequent consultations with national and international experts, interacted with regulators and policy makers, and provided rollout recommendations on priority groups for vaccination, optimal dosing intervals, vaccination of different population groups including children, pregnant and lactating mothers, immune-compromised individuals and

N. K. Arora (✉) · R. Shrivas
The INCLEN Trust International, New Delhi, India
e-mail: nkarora@inclentrust.org

A. K. Singh
NIHFW, New Delhi, India

Department of Epidemiology, School of Public Health, University of Michigan, Ann Arbor, MI, USA

D. Kumar · K. Duggal · K. Bhaattacharyya
NIHFW, New Delhi, India

M. Agnani et al. (eds.), *India's Covid-19 Vaccine Drive*,
https://doi.org/10.1007/978-981-95-8138-2_2

indications for booster/protection doses. CWG regularly reviewed the AEFI (Adverse Event Following Immunization) data for vaccine safety to allay community concerns. CWG recommended data harmonization and synthesis across activities and sectors. The timely, transparent and evidence-based recommendations from CWG/NTAGI facilitated efficient and timely policy decisions by Ministry of Health and Family Welfare, contributing significantly to the reduction in severe cases, hospitalizations, and mortality. Overall NTAGI contributed and complimented in a significant manner to the overall national endeavours of managing the pandemic.

Keywords
National Technical Advisory Group (NTAGI) · Standing Technical Subcommittee (STSC) · Covid-19 Working Group (CWG) · Covid-19 vaccines · Vaccination strategy · Transparency · Evidence based · Recommendation · Program performance · Vaccine R&D · Pandemic preparedness

2.1 Introduction

Vaccines are one of the best public health tools to prevent substantial amount of morbidity and mortality around the world. They play a crucial role in managing pandemics by modifying disease course, reducing severity, reducing transmission, and providing protective immunity. In past 50 years, global immunization efforts have saved almost 154 million lives [13]. The Covid-19 vaccination had substantially reduced the hospitalization and death rates across the world [8, 9].

Most Covid-19 deaths occurred during the pre-vaccine era and the Delta wave of the Covid-19 pandemic. With the identification of first Covid-19 case in the country, the Government of India took a swift decision to invest significantly in Covid-19 vaccine R&D and manufacturer in the country. Several science departments including ICMR and DBT made special task forces to achieve the national objectives. This was also the time when nationwide steps were taken to augment public health systems. This was the reason that India was able to introduce on 16 January 2021 two 'Made-in-India' vaccines, within 5 weeks of the first global introduction of the Covid-19 vaccines elsewhere.

2.2 The National Technical Advisory Group on Immunization

The National Technical Advisory Group on Immunisation (NTAGI) was established by an order of the Ministry of Health and Family Welfare (MoHFW) in 2001. As India's apex advisory body on immunization, the NTAGI provides guidance and advice to the MoHFW on provision of vaccination and immunization services for the effective control of vaccine preventable diseases in the country [4].

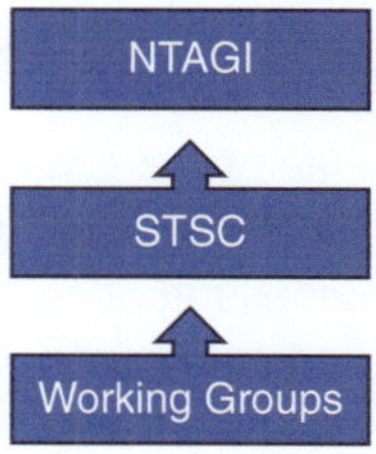

Fig. 2.1 Three tier evidence review structure of the NTAGI

The overall objective of the NTAGI is to provide advice to the MoHFW on the strategies to control the vaccine preventable burden and appropriately evaluate the impact of immunization in the country.

The NTAGI evaluates licensed vaccines as well as other related interventions such as immune globulins and chemo-prophylactic agents and new technologies for delivery, logistics, disease prevention and monitoring of VPD prevalence, vaccination programme and other adjuncts to control VPD. If circumstances necessitate the use of unlicensed vaccines, NTAGI is expected to develop guidance on their use considering the risks and benefits to the population.

The NTAGI is supported by Standing Technical Subcommittee (STSC) for an in-depth evaluation of the evidence. On need basis, subject matter working groups are formed to support NTAGI-STSC (Fig. 2.1).

2.3 Covid-19 Working Group (CWG)

In view of the enormity of the challenges of Covid-19 pandemic and immunization-related tasks, particularly the need for speedy decision making during the course of pandemic was foreseen by chairs of NTAGI and STSC and a formal Covid-19 working group (CWG) was constituted in July 2020. The task of the group was to support swift decision making through review and synthesize of rapidly emerging and changing scientific evidence and data on epidemiology, disease severity, vaccine research and development, real world vaccine effectiveness, selection of vaccines, vaccine safety and hesitancy, recipient prioritization and program preparation for vaccine rollout and associated logistics. CWG was also the platform that brought together key stakeholders like DBT, ICMR, NCDC, DCGI, WHO and Unicef regularly to share their activities, data and proposed next steps. CWG member(s) regularly attended National Empowered Group (NEG) on Immunization that took policy decisions. The CWG invited global experts and Covid-19 vaccine innovators as special invitees for clarification of ambivalent scientific and programmatic issues first hand.

The Covid-19 working group comprised globally renowned experts in the area of vaccinology, infectious disease, epidemiology, public health, immunology, molecular biology, immunization program and regulatory system. The Covid-19 WG met 53 times spanning across the pandemic period and provided guidance on multiple scientific issues of public policy and program importance.

2.4 Interaction with Regulator

One of the CWG members was the regulator (DCGI (Drug Controller General of India)). It became amply clear early that vaccine will be a key tool to counter the damaging effects of the pandemic, and regulatory pathways will have to be modified to access new products in a timely manner without compromising the critical issues of safety and efficacy. CWG gave its suggestions when guidelines and process of granting emergency use authorization (EUA) were being framed by the CDSCO. CWG discussed regulatory issues of pre-clinical studies, phase 1, 2 and 3 study designs, immunogenicity, value of bridging studies in the context of pandemic, safety and efficacy criteria, post-EUA pharmaco-vigilance, impact on vulnerable populations and challenges of regulatory compliances by the manufacturers. CWG asked for additional pre-clinical and clinical data from the manufacturers through regulators to get convinced about the processes and interpretation of the findings.

2.5 Vaccine Development and Emergency Use Authorization

The science of vaccine R&D has evolved substantially in past two decades, resulting in several new platforms available for the development of new vaccines. Strategic and robust national and international scientific collaborations were seen during the pandemic for the development of the vaccines [3]. Critical infrastructure required for vaccine development existed with in the country. Government of India invested heavily in the R&D and manufacture of Covid-19 vaccines in India as part of 'Atmanirbhar Bharat' philosophy soon after the first case of Covid-19 was reported in the country. Vaccine R&D projects were supported by DBT, ICMR and other science departments; special efforts were made to marshal vaccine experts from both national and international institutions and projects executed in partnership between academia and industry. These platforms included mRNA, viral vector, DNA, protein subunit, live attenuated and whole cell killed vaccines, nasal vaccine and others. Globally, the Pfizer-BioNTech mRNA Covid-19 vaccine was the first vaccine licenced by the FDA, USA, under emergency use authorization (EUA) in December 2020. In India, the DCGI, Central Drugs Standard Control Organisation (CDSCO) authorized two Covid-19 vaccines: COVISHIELD™—a viral vector based vaccine and COVAXIN™—a whole cell killed vaccine for restricted use in emergency situation (EUA) in January 2021. Series of pre-clinical and phase 1, 2 and 3 clinical studies for all the Covid-19 vaccines under development in India were reviewed by CWG for study quality, vaccine efficacy and safety including potential for vaccine-associated enhanced disease (VAED). Additionally there were immunogenicity and safety studies for determining appropriate homologous and heterologous booster/protection dose, protection by the vaccines developed with ancestral strain against emerging Covid-19 mutants (variants of concern-VOC; variants under monitoring (VUM)) and safety studies for children for some of the vaccines given EUA. Pivotal phase 3 trial for two Indian vaccines, namely, COVAXIN™ and Zycov-D™ comprised of over 25 thousand subjects; for other vaccines, bridging trials in 3000–4000 subjects were conducted. Through the pandemic period, following 'Made-in-India' vaccines were also authorized for restricted use in emergency situation: vectored vaccine (Sputnik-V™, Sputnik-light™), protein sub-unit vaccine (Corbevax™ and Covovax™), DNA vaccine (ZyCov-D™), mRNA vaccine (GEMCOVAC-19™ and GEMCOVAC-OM™) and nasal vectored vaccine (iNCOVACC™). Scientific evidence reviewed by the Covid-19 working group (CWG) of the NTAGI was then presented to the STSC for making recommendations to the NTAGI and Ministry of Health and Family Welfare for timely public health action.

2.6 Scientific Criteria for Importing Covid-19 Vaccines

In view of the limited indigenous Covid-19 vaccine availability during the first half of 2021, Indian regulatory authorities CDSCO intended fast tracked approval of international vaccines with specific regulatory profile. The CWG undertook extensive review of the available literature of the Covid-19 vaccines being used at that time in different parts of the world. Factors for down selecting vaccines included evidence on serological response with appropriate neutralizing antibody response and more than 50% efficacy in clinical trials or effectiveness in real world and vaccines with large number of doses (e.g., more than 100 million) administered elsewhere, without any safety signals and benefits outweighed risks. Vaccines that had received WHO emergency use listing and that had received EUA from regulatory authority of any of the following countries/agencies: USA, UK, Japan or EMA were to be considered for import. For these vaccines, the CWG-NTAGI recommended waiving of bridging studies. Programmatic feasibility issues, e.g. cold chain requirements, storage, transport and administration, were also considered while deciding to import the vaccines [5].

2.7 Mapping the Burden of the Covid-19 in India

The CWG consistently monitored national and regional data on following throughout the pandemic:

- State-wise number of cases and deaths: CWG regularly reviewed the Covid-19 infection testing data (RT-PCR/other techniques) (portal maintained by ICMR) and clinical, epidemiology, death and hospitalization data (portal maintained by MOHFW/NCDC) by age, comorbidities and geographies. Nation-wide sentinel surveillance was established for detecting Covid-19 positivity in ILI (influenza-like illness) patients. Sample positivity rate was reviewed regularly for intensity of the viral transmission in different parts of the country.
- Age stratified fatality and hospitalization and severity association with specific variants of concern (VOC)

- Sero surveys: data from national and local surveys for monitoring the spread of the pandemic
- Modelling exercises by different institutions and academic groups to determine the burden, predictions about spread of the infections/disease and need for additional health infrastructure
- Circulation of Covid-19 variants at different time points as per the Indian SARS-CoV-2 Genomics Consortium (INSACOG)

2.8 Prioritization of the Population for Covid-19 Vaccine

It became quite clear that earliest batches of Indian Covid-19 vaccines would probably be available in first quarter of 2021. During initial few months, the availability of the vaccine doses was likely to be restricted and therefore recipient prioritization was necessary. Based on detailed discussion and deliberations, the recipient prioritization was made by the CWG group in October 2020, which was revisable in the light of emerging evidences and increased availability of vaccine doses [2]. Following six principles that were part of WHO-SAGE's vaccine allocation guidelines were given consideration while making a prioritization framework: societal value, equity of vaccine access, societal reciprocity, evidence-based transparent decision making and involvement of all stake holders.

With augmented manufacturing capacities, the availability of number of vaccine doses increased, and from 1 May 2021, the primary Covid-19 vaccination was unlocked for the whole adult population (>18 years old).

2.9 Interval Between Two Doses of Primary Series of Covid-19 Vaccines

COVAXIN™ is inactivated viral vaccine, and the two primary doses were given at 4-week interval. This interval was the consistent recommendation for COVAXIN™ as well for other international killed viral vaccines. Although there were publications about the need for third primary dose for inactivated viral vaccines from some international manufacturers, the immunogenicity data about COVAXIN™ did not suggest for such change in the recommendation for the Indian vaccine. However, for COVISHIELD™, the global evidence on differences between the effectiveness and durability of protection of short interval (4–6 weeks) versus long interval (8–12 weeks) was reviewed and deliberated by the CWG and STSC. The original phase 3 trial data suggested that disease protection with dose interval of 4 weeks versus 12 weeks was 55%–60% and 80%–82%, respectively; maximum when interval was more than 12 weeks. South-East Asia region, Bangladesh and Sri Lanka used more than 8 weeks or 10 weeks of interval between two doses of COVISHIELD™. EMA (European Medical Agency) had recommended an interval of 4–12 weeks [10]. The Chair of the WHO-Strategic Advisory Group of Experts (SAGE) and the Chair of the Joint committee on Vaccine and Immunization (JCVI),

UK, were invited to provide their expert viewpoints. After reviewing all available evidence and in-depth deliberations, interval between two primary doses was raised from 4–6 to 12–16 weeks [10]. This was expected to increased protection by ~20%–25%. Later studies demonstrated that increased primary dose interval for COVISHIELD™ was associated with sustained protection beyond 6 months with fewer breakthrough infections, reduced hospitalization among fully immunized individuals particularly during Delta wave, and higher levels of neutralizing antibodies and T-cell responses.

2.10 Covid-19 Vaccination for Pregnant Women

As per the standard trial guidelines, pregnant and lactating women were excluded from the early Covid-19 vaccine clinical trials globally and in India as well. In the pandemic situation, it was observed that the pregnant women were at higher risk of severe Covid-19 disease and increased possibility of preterm deliveries and stillbirth. Some of the international vaccine manufacturers had done pre-clinical DART (developmental and reproductive toxicology) studies to determine the safety of the vaccine in pregnant women. In India, only Biologic E had undertaken DART studies for their Covid-19 protein subunit vaccine available during the latter part of the pandemic. However, real-life experience was available in pregnant women for different vaccines internationally including adenovirus vectored (AstraZeneca/COVISHIELD™) and inactivated virus vaccines (Chinese vaccines: Sinopharma; Sinovac). Therefore, the CWG-NTAGI deliberated on the issue and recommended the following in July 2021 [5]:

(a) The Covid-19 vaccine could be given anytime during the pregnancy. All pregnant women visiting for antenatal care or the Covid-19 vaccination Centres (CVC) were to be informed about the risks and benefits associated with the Covid-19 vaccines (COVISHIELD™ and COVAXIN™) available in the country. Pregnant woman were offered the available Covid-19 vaccine at the nearest CVC.
(b) All lactating women would be eligible to receive the Covid-19 vaccines any time after delivery.
(c) NTAGI instructed to initiate studies to monitor the safety of COVISHIELD™ and COVAXIN™ among pregnant women.

An educational tool comprising information on the risk of Covid-19 infection during pregnancy, benefits associated with the Covid-19 vaccination and rare complications associated with vaccines, e.g. thrombosis thrombocytopenia syndrome (TTS), was developed and communicated to pregnant women before administering the vaccine. Since previously published evidence indicated established safety profile of inactivated viral vaccine in pregnant women, COVAXIN™ was considered the first choice in pregnant women as per availability.

2.11 Covid-19 Vaccination for Immune-Compromised

The clinical trials data on Covid-19 vaccines that led to their emergency use authorization had limited number of immune-compromised people. Due to impaired immune response to vaccination and infection, they remained vulnerable to heavy viral load and severe complications [7]. Definition of immune-compromised was developed for guiding the program implementation. This was applicable for both primary and booster/protection dose recipients. Immune-compromised were prioritized for initial recipient of the Covid-19 vaccines at the time of vaccine rollout. CWG recommended that a third dose should be offered to individuals aged ≥18 years with moderate to severe immunosuppression for completion of the primary schedule [11].

2.12 Break Through Infection and Covid-19 Vaccine Tracking Platform

Breakthrough infections are those infections, which occurred 2 weeks after getting the second dose or full schedule of the vaccine. It was strongly recommended to establish a National Vaccine tracking platform to determine the impact of Covid-19 vaccines and track breakthrough infections. A team was constituted to work on harmonization of Covid-19 India portal data for infections, ICMR Covid-19 testing portal data and CoWIN data for vaccine tracking.

2.13 Covid-19 Booster/Protection Shots

The booster dose was also labelled as protection dose in India. The issue of booster dose was deliberated at CWG in the third quarter of 2021 in the context of WHO-SAGE recommendations and experience from other countries. The CWG recommended to STSC that booster/protection doses were not required for general population due to hybrid immunity (large proportion of population naturally infected and over 90% adults had received both primary doses) and gradually declining number of both symptomatic and severe Covid-19 cases [11]. In view of these, the NTAGI recommended and emphasized to focus booster/protection doses specifically in elderly individuals (>60 years), immune-compromised/immune-suppressed, individuals with comorbidities (including TB patients, those with disabilities) and malignancies. Booster/protection doses for whole 18+ population were introduced in January 2022 because the identification of high risk population in programmatic settings was challenging. The initial recommendation for interval between primary schedule and booster/protection dose was 9 months which was later changed to 6 months aligning with global guidelines, and for health personnel, the booster could be administered 3 months after completion of the primary schedule. Studies of homologous and heterologous booster/protection doses and interchangeability of available vaccines were also initiated, and CWG reviewed these studies for immune responses and safety. STSC and NTAGI recommended diverse combinations of heterologous booster/protection doses (as the additional Indian vaccines received EUA) and recommended monitoring of real world safety through systematic post-marketing pharmaco-vigilance studies [6]. Ancestral strain of SARS-CoV-2 virus had mutated several times by end of 2021, and Omicron strain and its variants had appeared. In 2023, the first Omicron-specific mRNA vaccine was given EUA for use as booster/protection dose.

2.14 Covid-19 Vaccination for Under 18 Population

During the pandemic, the data consistently showed that only 5% to 6% of the total hospitalizations were in the children. The deaths in the paediatric age group (≤18 years) accounted for less than 1%–2% of the total deaths; most of these were in 12–17 year old. Based on the available evidence, the risk of severe disease and mortality due to Covid-19 disease in children was more in the following associated comorbid conditions:

- Type 1 Diabetes receiving insulin therapy
- Heart diseases: Congenital/rheumatic
- Immune-compromised/immune-deficient patients
- Children with chronic kidney disease
- Children with chronic liver disease
- Morbid/severe obesity (adult equivalent for morbid obesity: BMI >40 kg/m^2; severe obesity: BMI >35)
- Neuro-developmental disorders
- Chronic respiratory diseases: Uncontrolled severe persistent asthma and chronic lung diseases (interstitial lung disease/cystic fibrosis)

Again due to challenges of identifying and labelling children with co-morbidities in program settings, Covid-19 vaccines were recommended for children of age 12–17 years age in January 2022. NTAGI did not recommend Covid-19 vaccines for children less than 12 years old because few serious consequences of the pandemic were observed in them [6]. Due to safety reasons, COVISHIELD™ was not recommended for paediatric age group. The other EUA vaccines available in the country that had done studies in children were permitted. COVAXIN™ and CARBEVAX™ were administered to 12- to 17-year-old children in the national Covid-19-vaccination program.

2.15 Covid-19 Vaccination Program Review and Guidance

The Immunization Division regularly presented the program status to CWG and sought guidance on Covid-19 vaccine-related indications and some of the program operating processes. NTAGI developed travel and quarantine guidance during the pandemic. NTAGI recommended to include the names of individuals who had travelled internationally and had received Covid-19 vaccines outside the country on CO-WIN IT platform after due verification of name of the vaccine, doses received and dates. For vaccine recipients, the following guidance were provided:

- Individuals who wanted to donate blood; they were advised to do so only after 15 days of the last dose of the of Covid-19 vaccine.
- Next dose of Covid-19 vaccine was to be deferred in the following situations and for the period as specified:
  - 26 weeks (6 months) after receipt of plasma therapy/monoclonal antibodies
  - 4–6 weeks after discharge from hospitalization due to any reason
  - 12 weeks (3 months) post-covid-19 recovery; only clinical recovery is to be considered and RT-PCR based evidence was not required
  - In case of breakthrough Covid-19 infection after the first dose of the vaccine, second dose was to be deferred for at least 3 months after clinical recovery.

2.16 Covid-19 Vaccine Safety Surveillance

Once a vaccine gets approval or authorization for use, vaccine safety eco system, including national AEFI surveillance program, monitors serious and severe adverse events and also expected to look for safety signals [1, 12]. Since the introduction of Covid-19 vaccines into the program, the CWG, STSC and NTAGI regularly examined the AEFI data and based on the observations recommended further Covid-19 vaccine safety studies, especially in pregnant women [5, 6]. The AEFI data was closely scrutinized for TTS following Covid-19 vaccines particularly COVISHIELD™. Some of the suspected TTS cases were extensively reviewed by CWG.

2.17 Identification of Evidence Gaps and Encouraging Policy and Program Relevant Research

Throughout the Covid-19 pandemic, the CWG, STSC and NTAGI consistently deliberated about existing and emerging evidence gaps that were of R&D, programmatic and operational nature and significant for developing effective countermeasures. Several basic science research questions emerged and were important for fast moving vaccine R&D taking place in the country. These included but not restricted to: preparation of local reference standards for immunologic assays; establishment and strengthening measurement of in vitro and in vivo T and B cell responses; vaccine sparing strategies, vaccine effectiveness in the light of rapidly emerging new variants of concern, interchangeability of vaccines, health conditions requiring additional doses for primary dose schedule, homologous and heterologous booster studies for effectiveness and safety to mention a few. The challenge of reaching 1.4

billion and delivery of the Covid-19 vaccines within a very short period was not an easy task. Similarly program had to develop strategies for accessing diagnostic facilities for Covid-19 infection in every part of the country. Data science and informatics was central for continual measurement of burden of the entire spectrum of Covid-19 disease, impact of immunization on restricting the consequences of the pandemic on population health and health system, and the modelling exercises to predict infection dynamics in the country. For this purpose, vaccine tracker was established to determine real-life impact of vaccination, and recommendations were made to link and harmonize data sets from different sources and platforms.

The research questions and need for generating evidence were shared with academics, national and international funding agencies, philanthropies, industry and private sector. It was heartening that evidence generation was catalysed and evidence-driven decision making heavily influenced India's fight against the Covid-19 pandemic.

2.18 Lessons Learned and Future Directions

The Covid-19 pandemic posed unprecedented scientific, programmatic and governance challenges globally; timely decision making was the key to guide public health action. NTAGI through its working arms STSC and CWG provided critical technical and programmatic inputs for the Covid-19 immunization program throughout the pandemic. To address the rapidly evolving situation, dedicated Covid-19 Working Group (CWG) was constituted in July 2020. CWG reviewed scientific evidence and program data on epidemiology, disease severity, vaccine research and development, real world vaccine effectiveness, vaccine safety and hesitancy and program preparation for vaccine rollout and associated logistics and provided timely recommendations. This was an important and strategic decision and provides important lesson for all future emergencies and pandemics. The timely, transparent and evidence-based recommendations from NTAGI-STSC-CWG facilitated efficient and prompt policy decisions by Ministry of Health and Family Welfare, contributing significantly to the reduction in severe cases, hospitalizations and mortality, service delivery that was equity centred and notably maintained community confidence on the Covid-19 countermeasures in general and immunization program in particular. NTAGI provided additional layer of quality assurance beyond CDSCO/regulators and regularly reviewed the pre-clinical and clinical vaccine R&D data. CWG generated relevant research agenda for continuous refinement and mid-course correction of the immunization program. Large-scale employment of IT and application of principles of the data science were innovative and transformative; however, more attention was required for data harmonization and synthesis across activities and sectors. Overall NTAGI contributed and complimented in a significant manner to the overall national endeavours of managing the pandemic.

References

1. Centre for Disease Control. COVID-19 vaccine safety reporting systems. 2024. Retrieved September 19, 2024, from https://www.cdc.gov/vaccine-safety-systems/monitoring/covid-19.html.
2. CWG, N. S. Preliminary guidance document on use of COVID-19 vaccines in India. New Delhi. 2020.
3. Kuter BJ, Offit PA, Poland GA. The development of COVID-19 vaccines in the United States: why and how so fast? Vaccine. 2021;39:2491–5.
4. Ministry of Health and Family Welfare, Government of India. NTAGI code of practice July 2015 final. New Delhi: Ministry of Health & Family Welfare, Government of India; 2015. Retrieved from papers 3. https://www.mohfw.gov.in/sites/default/files/CODE_OF_PRACTICE.pdf.
5. NTAGI, N. S. Sixteenth NTAGI meeting. New Delhi. 2021.
6. NTAGI, N. S. Seventeenth NTAGI meeting. New Delhi. 2022.
7. Shoham S, Batista C, Ben Amor Y, Ergonul O, Hassanain M, Hotez P, et al. Vaccines and therapeutics for immunocompromised patients with COVID-19. EClinicalMedicine. 2023;59:101965. https://doi.org/10.1016/j.eclinm.2023.101965.
8. Singh P, Anand A, Rana S, Kumar A, Goel P, Kumar S, et al. Impact of COVID-19 vaccination: a global perspective. Front Public Health. 2023;11(January):1–10. https://doi.org/10.3389/fpubh.2023.1272961.
9. Steele MK, Couture A, Reed C, Iuliano D, Whitaker M, Fast H, et al. Estimated number of COVID-19 infections, hospitalizations, and deaths prevented among vaccinated persons in the US, December 2020 to September 2021. JAMA Netw Open. 2022;5(7):E2220385. https://doi.org/10.1001/jamanetworkopen.2022.20385.
10. STSC, N. S. Thirty-first STSC meeting. New Delhi. 2021.
11. STSC, N. S. Thirty-sixth STSC meeting. New Delhi. 2021.
12. World Health Organization. Establishing surveillance systems in countries using COVID-19 vaccines. Covid-19 vaccines: safety surveillance manual. World Health Organization; 2020.
13. World Health Organization. Global immunization efforts have saved at least 154 million lives over the past 50 years. World Health Organization; 2024. Retrieved from https://www.who.int/news/item/24-04-2024-global-immunization-efforts-have-saved-at-least-154-million-lives-over-the-past-50-years.

Prioritization of Beneficiaries for Covid-19 Vaccination

3

Ashish Chauhan

Abstract

Early in the Covid-19 pandemic, vaccines emerged to be significantly effective in protecting against Covid-19. Their efficacy led to a disproportionate gap in demand and supply of vaccines, which mandated the need for staggered introduction of vaccines by prioritizing the vulnerable population to maximize the benefits of available vaccines. In India, this prioritization was done by the National Expert Group on Vaccine Administration for Covid-19 (NEGVAC) to ensure equitable distribution of vaccines across population groups that were prioritized based on risk factors and a focus on achieving public health goals. The rollout began with safeguarding healthcare and front-line workers who were involved in pandemic management. Subsequent phases addressed age, comorbidities, and physiological condition of beneficiaries while keeping a constant watch on vaccine availability, existing and emerging evidence, and the capacity of the healthcare system. With vigilance and integrity, the endeavour of prioritization achieved equitable access to vaccines while prioritizing those at highest risk.

Keywords

Covid-19 · Vaccine · NEGVAC · NTAGI · Prioritization · Age · Precaution dose

A. Chauhan (✉)
UNICEF, New Delhi, India
e-mail: achauhan@unicef.org

M. Agnani et al. (eds.), *India's Covid-19 Vaccine Drive*,
https://doi.org/10.1007/978-981-95-8138-2_3

The novelty of Covid-19 disease had posed a significant challenge in terms of unavailability of any vaccine against it. Within months of identification of Covid-19 virus, multiple research institutes across the globe had put in efforts to create a vaccine against it. Their efforts had yielded positive outcomes with hundreds of vaccine candidates being tested in pre-clinical and clinical phases of development.

Manufacturers like Pfizer, Moderna and AstraZeneca were amongst the first to develop a safe and effective vaccine against Covid-19, which were approved after rigorous clinical trials. Indian manufacturer Bharat Biotech was not far behind, and the vaccine developed and manufactured by it was also approved. The approval of these vaccines within approximately a year of identification of Covid-19 virus was a testament of excellence achieved by science and technology.

However, the demand for vaccines was across the world and the manufacturing units were handful. Amid the series of lockdowns, restrictions, and disruption, every individual, every community, every country wanted to get the vaccine and resume the pre-Covid-19 life. This highly disproportionate gap in demand and supply of vaccines mandated that a 'triage' like system be introduced and implemented to maximize the benefits of available vaccines.

Further, National Expert Group on Vaccine Administration for Covid-19 (NEGVAC) was constituted in August 2020, to formulate a comprehensive action plan for vaccine administration. NEGVAC was co-chaired by Member (Health) NITI Aayog and Union Health Secretary. It had representation of Secretaries from the Ministry of External Affairs, Departments of Expenditure, Biotechnology, Health Research, Pharmaceuticals, Ministry of Electronics and Information Technology, representatives from five State Governments (Assam, Madhya Pradesh, Maharashtra, Tamil Nadu, and Uttar Pradesh on periodic basis) and technical experts. Terms of Reference of NEGVAC were to provide guidance on the following:

1. Conceptualization and Implementation Mechanisms for Digital Infrastructure:
   - Develop a digital inventory management system that tracks vaccine stock levels, expiration dates, and distribution to vaccination sites.
   - Implement a real-time tracking system for the vaccination process, including monitoring doses administered and adverse events following immunization (AEFI).
   - Utilize mobile applications or online platforms for appointment scheduling and tracking of individuals vaccinated till the last mile.
2. Selection of Covid-19 Vaccine Candidates:
   - Evaluate vaccine candidates based on safety, efficacy, and availability.
   - Consider recommendations from the National Expert Group and the Standing Technical Sub-Committee of NTAGI.
3. Procurement Mechanism of Covid-19 Vaccine:
   - Establish a procurement strategy for both indigenous and international vaccines.
   - Ensure transparency and fairness in the procurement process.

4. Prioritization of Population Groups for Vaccination:
    - Develop a prioritization framework based on risk factors, including age, occupation, and underlying health conditions.
    - Ensure equitable distribution of vaccines across priority groups.
5. Financial Resources for Vaccine Procurement:
    - Estimate the financial resources required for vaccine procurement based on the selected candidates and population targets.
    - Explore various financing options, including government budgets, external funding, and partnerships.
6. Selection of Delivery Platforms and Cold Chain Infrastructure:
    - Identify suitable delivery platforms, such as health centres, mobile vaccination units, and outreach programs.
    - Strengthen cold chain infrastructure to ensure the safe storage and transportation of vaccines.
7. Equitable and Transparent Vaccine Delivery:
    - Develop contingency plans for various scenarios, such as vaccine shortages, logistical challenges, and adverse events.
    - Ensure transparency in vaccine distribution and prioritize vulnerable populations.
8. Vaccine Safety and Surveillance:
    - Establish a robust system for monitoring and reporting AEFIs.
    - Follow the recommendations of the National AEFI Committee for vaccine safety.
9. Creating Awareness and Disseminating Information:
    - Launch a comprehensive communication campaign to raise awareness about the Covid-19 vaccines.
    - Provide accurate and timely information on vaccine safety, efficacy, and availability.
10. Supporting Neighbouring and Partner Countries:
    - Collaborate with international organizations and partners to support Covid-19 vaccination efforts in neighbouring and partner countries.
    - Share expertise and resources to enhance global vaccine access.
11. Leveraging Domestic Vaccine Manufacturing Capacity:
    - Support domestic vaccine manufacturers to ramp up production of Covid-19 vaccines for national and international supply.
    - Collaborate with international partners to facilitate technology transfer and capacity building.

These strategies were implemented in coordination with relevant stakeholders, including government agencies, healthcare providers, and community organizations, to ensure a successful and equitable Covid-19 vaccination campaign.

Overall, NEGVAC's guidance was instrumental in shaping India's Covid-19 vaccination strategy and ensuring the effective and efficient rollout of the vaccination program.

India already had an apex body of experts called National Technical Advisory Group on Immunization (NTAGI). It was established in August 2001 with an aim to provide technical advice for all aspects of the Universal Immunization Programme. NTAGI is chaired by the Secretary, Health & Family Welfare and co-chaired by Secretary, Department of Biotechnology and Secretary, Department of Health Research, who is also Director General of Indian Council of Medical Research (ICMR). Other members are eminent experts from fields of Public Health, Microbiology, Health Research and Paediatricians across the country, and professional bodies like Indian Academy of Pediatrics, National Centre for Disease Control (NCDC) and officials from Ministry of Health & Family Welfare.

NTAGI reviews the available evidence on the disease burden, available preventive, and control measures; cost-effectiveness of available vaccine in preventing the disease under consideration and based on it recommends the vaccine for introduction in the Universal Immunization Programme. Following the recommendation of NTAGI, the proposal for new vaccine introduction is approved by the Mission Steering Group of National Health Mission under the chairpersonship of Union Minister of Health & Family Welfare, before the vaccine is introduced in the UIP.

Since its constitution, NTAGI has contributed to introduction of various new vaccines, namely, Hepatitis B vaccine, Japanese Encephalitis vaccine, Pentavalent Vaccine, Rotavirus vaccine, Pneumococcal Conjugate Vaccine and Inactivated Polio Vaccine. It has also recommended introduction of auto-disabled syringes in the programme. Besides the introduction of these vaccines, the dosage schedule of vaccine has also been recommended and at times revised (JE, MCV, IPV) based on scientific evidence.

The scope of activities of NTAGI includes the following:

- The decision to introduce any new vaccine in Universal Immunization Programme.
- Guidance on off-label use of vaccines at dosage schedule or age-group that might be different from the one for which it is approved. However, any such decision goes through a stringent review of scientific evidence.
- Guidance on all matters related to immunization policy and programmes including the circumstances (e.g., pandemics, natural disaster, etc.) in which a vaccine or related agent is recommended.
- The National Technical Advisory Group on Immunization (NTAGI) is represented in the National Expert Group on Vaccine Administration for Covid-19 (NEGVAC). NTAGI, through its Standing Technical Sub-committee (STSC) and Covid-19 Working Group, has been providing technical advice to NEGVAC on various aspects of Covid-19 vaccination. This includes advice on dosage inter-

vals, contraindications, vaccination of specific groups such as pregnant and lactating women, adverse event following immunization (AEFI) surveillance, and other technical matters related to Covid-19 vaccination.

It is important to note that NTAGI and NEGVAC are programme-specific bodies assisting the decision making. However, it is the Central Drugs Standards Control Organization (CDSCO), an autonomous body that reviews the evidence of clinical trials of all vaccines and drugs and based on these data and approves or disapproves use of any vaccine in the country. Every batch of vaccine is tested at the CDSCO laboratories before being released in the market for its use.

In a normal situation, these organizations work sequentially but given the unprecedented pandemic that was fought against, these three bodies worked parallelly to analyse emerging evidence that would enable to finalize the country's strategy for Covid-19 vaccination. During clinical trials of vaccines, both NEGVAC and NTAGI were closely keeping an eye on the advances of clinical trials these vaccine candidates were making and the production capacities of these companies.

Once approved, the real challenge was ahead as to who should get the vaccine first. The public health goals to be achieved by way of Covid-19 vaccination included the following:

1. Prevent infection
2. Prevent disease
3. Prevent hospital admission
4. Prevent ICU admission
5. Prevent death
6. Prevent transmission

Since the Covid-19 was a new disease, the number of manufacturers of Covid-19 vaccine remained limited despite unprecedented thrust on research and development of vaccines. Hence, the availability of vaccines remained limited amidst huge demand thereby creating a demand-supply gap.

All the goals of vaccination could not be achieved at once in the face of limited availability of the vaccine. It was only rational that the priority public health goals are clarified upfront for determining the prioritization of vaccination strategy in phases. These goals changed with time in tandem with the dynamic situation of the pandemic and of vaccine availability.

During the initial phase of vaccine production, only a limited supply was available. Hence, population groups who would receive the vaccine in this phase would have to be prioritized to maximize the impact of vaccination drive on ongoing pandemic.

With the background work already done in terms of vaccine availability, it was most prudent to first vaccinate the protectors of the society. Cognizant of the manufacturing capacity, the population of the country, scientific evidence, and global best practices, NEGVAC recommended that the first shot of vaccines be made available to those who were taking care of the sick along with those who were the guardians of civilization in those testing times. Hence, the first priority was identified as protecting India's Pandemic Response System (Healthcare & Front-Line Workers), since it formed the foundation of any nation's capacity to manage and mitigate the pandemic.

This recommendation of NEGVAC was implemented, and most of the Health Care Workers and Front-Line Workers received their dose of vaccine within 45 days of the vaccination drive. These groups included healthcare providers and workers in both public and private healthcare settings, as well as Integrated Child Development Scheme (ICDS) workers. Frontline workers comprised personnel from state and central police departments, armed forces, home guards, civil defence organizations (including disaster management volunteers), municipal workers (excluding healthcare workers), staff from Panchayati Raj Institutions (PRI), revenue staff involved in containment and surveillance, Railway Protection Force (RPF) personnel, and poll officials.

Once the decision of inclusion of various cadres of workers as Health Care Workers and Front-Line Workers was taken, the next big challenge was to create a database of all these workers for vaccination. To achieve this, the various departments and ministries managing these employees were contacted and their organogram understood. Then the user-id and passwords for Co-WIN were created in a hierarchical manner with some IDs for entering the database in required format and some IDs for approval. The training of all these stakeholders was conducted by MoHFW, and a helpline was also established to support them in creating the database of all the Health Care Workers and Front-Line Workers. The vaccination of all these workers was done using Co-WIN software, and within 45 days of launch of vaccination programme, a vast majority of these workers had received their first dose of Covid-19 vaccine.

Based on the analysis of Covid-19 deaths and the vaccination progress, NEGVAC decided that the second priority for Covid-19 vaccination should focus on controlling the vulnerability and mortality risks associated with the disease. This decision was made considering that a significant proportion of the first priority group had received one dose of the Covid-19 vaccine and that there had been an improvement in vaccine manufacturing capacity. The analysis of Covid-19 deaths in India revealed that 54% of all deaths occurred among individuals above 60 years of age, while those in the 50–59 age group accounted for 24% of deaths. Additionally, it was estimated that more than 80% of all deaths occurred in individuals aged 45 years and above. These findings underscored the importance of prioritizing vaccination for older age groups to reduce mortality and vulnerability to Covid-19. The analysis of Covid-19 mortality further shows that 67% of deaths occur in those who have one or more significant co-morbidity such as diabetes, heart disease, renal failure, chronic pulmonary disease, etc. Hence, protecting individuals with serious co-morbidities at any age was critical to reduce deaths due to Covid-19 disease.

The prioritization criteria for Covid-19 vaccination from the World Health Organization (WHO) and other countries, such as the UK, France, and the USA, emphasized a stepwise, layered approach. For example, the UK initially prioritized vaccination for those aged 80 years and above, followed by those aged 75–79, then those aged 70–74, and so on, before eventually opening up vaccination to all eligible beneficiaries. France similarly prioritized vaccination for those aged 75 years and older, followed by the 65–74 age group, and eventually expanded to include all eligible individuals. In the USA, vaccination began with healthcare workers and higher age groups before becoming available to all adults. This approach ensured that those at highest risk of severe illness or death from Covid-19 were vaccinated first, gradually expanding eligibility to cover broader population groups. It was fairly evident that a staggered approach had been taken by countries starting with those with higher age group. India's approach was in consonance with WHO guidelines and International Practice in prioritization of population groups for Covid-19 vaccination.

It was estimated that in the 45–59 years age-group, around 8% of the population (roughly 2 crore population) had non-communicable diseases. The estimated number of health care workers and front-line workers that were prioritized for vaccination was approximately 3 crores. The age-group of 60 years and above were at highest risk of mortality and contributed around 13.75 crore beneficiaries, thereby taking the total number of beneficiaries to around 18.75 crore. This would have required availability of around 37.5 crore doses of Covid-19 vaccine to cover these beneficiaries with two dose regimes. With the forecast of vaccines being sufficient to cater to this group, the eligible beneficiaries were expanded from 1 March 2021 to persons above 60 years of age and persons above 45 years with associated specified 20 comorbidities. The above prioritization was based on principles of promoting public health (by preventing Covid-19-related illness and death, and protection of the health system), giving priority to the worst-off individuals (by addressing high mortality age-group) and reciprocity (by protecting those who face the increased risk of Covid-19 disease to provide essential services for the benefit of others).

Meanwhile various representations were received by the Ministry of Health and Family Welfare from various professional groups like Journalists, Lawyers, Public Elected representatives, etc., for including them as a prioritized group for Covid-19 vaccination.

However, the vaccination of Health Care Workers and Front-Line Workers remained on priority for sustaining the workforce involved in Covid-19 surveillance, containment, and management.

Further, as per the available scientific evidence, age was one of the most critical and clear indicators of increased risk to mortality followed by associated comorbidities. Any person from any professional group who was at an increased risk of mortality due to Covid-19 was being covered in the age-specific group or the group of associated co-morbidities. Inclusion of any group irrespective of their risk profile as a prioritized group would have led to inequitable distribution of Covid-19 vaccine.

An expert group of eminent doctors led by All India Institute of Medical Sciences (AIIMS), New Delhi, was constituted beforehand to identify the comorbidities with highest burden of mortality and morbidity due to Covid-19. The group recommended the following comorbidities to be prioritized for Covid-19 vaccination:

1. Heart failure with hospital admission in past 1 year
2. Post cardiac transplant/left ventricular assist device (LVAD)
3. Significant left ventricular systolic dysfunction (LVEF <40%)
4. Moderate or severe valvular heart disease
5. Congenital heart disease with severe PAH or idiopathic PAH
6. Coronary artery disease with past CABG/PTCA/MI AND hypertension/diabetes on treatment
7. Angina AND hypertension/diabetes on treatment
8. CT/MRI documented stroke AND hypertension/diabetes on treatment
9. Pulmonary artery hypertension AND hypertension/diabetes on treatment
10. Diabetes (>10 years OR with complications) AND hypertension on treatment
11. Kidney/liver/hematopoietic stem cell transplant: Recipient/on waitlist
12. End stage kidney disease on hemodialysis/CAPD
13. Current prolonged use of oral corticosteroids/immunosuppressant medications
14. Decompensated cirrhosis
15. Severe respiratory disease with hospitalizations in last 2 years/FEV1 <50%.
16. Lymphoma/leukaemia/myeloma
17. Diagnosis of any solid cancer on or after 1 July 2020 OR currently on any cancer therapy
18. Sickle cell disease/bone marrow failure/aplastic anaemia/thalassemia major
19. Primary immunodeficiency diseases/HIV infection
20. Persons with disabilities due to intellectual disabilities/muscular dystrophy/acid attack with involvement of respiratory system/persons with disabilities having high support needs/multiple disabilities including deaf, blindness.

At this time of Covid-19 vaccination, there was significant vaccine eagerness, and therefore, it was another challenge to verify that only those individuals with these comorbidities were vaccinated and no ineligible persons were getting vaccination out of turn. To achieve this, a format was designed which could be used by these patients to get their disease verified by their treating physician or any registered medical practitioner. This format was to be brought at the time of registration on Co-WIN software. However, it was soon realized that the verification system was not overtly citizen friendly and with the ever-improving vaccine availability, amid the prevalence of these 20 comorbidities, it was operationally prudent to remove the caveat of comorbidities and offer vaccination prioritized by age. Accordingly, the next phase of expansion of eligible population for Covid-19 vaccination, from 1 April 2021, saw inclusion of all people above 45 years of age.

While continuing with the above priority groups, considerations about vaccine security and the country's ability for administering this massive vaccination drive, from 1 May 2021, all other persons above 18 years of age were also made eligible for Covid-19 vaccination depending upon prioritization made by the respective State Governments and Union Territories, in view of their operational capacities. This criterion was further relaxed from 21 June 2021 when all persons aged 18 years and above, across the country, were made eligible for vaccination.

With ever relaxing eligibility criteria for vaccination, a very important cohort of pregnant and lactating women was missing out on vaccines because of lack of conclusive evidence of safety of these vaccines during pregnancy and lactation. It constituted a significant proportion of the population, but there were ethical concerns about vaccination amid lack of safety data despite Covid-19 infection having worse outcomes during pregnancy. This was because without establishing safety of vaccines in females without pregnancy and lactation, this group was not included in clinical trials. Once the safety in non-pregnant women was established, only then the pregnant women are included to know the effects of the vaccine on the foetus.

Amid growing demands from such mothers, their caretakers and opinions of renowned doctors, reasonable evidence was made available on the safety of vaccines in this group. The lactating women were made eligible for Covid-19 vaccination from 19 May 2021. However, the decision on inclusion of pregnant women needed more review of evidence as it was a higher risk situation as compared to lactation. NTAGI reviewed the evidence and following conclusions were made:

1. Pregnancy itself does not increase the risk to Covid-19 infection, but the evidence available at the time indicated that pregnant women are at an increased risk of severe illness from Covid-19 compared to non-pregnant women if they get infected.
2. Pregnant women infected with Covid-19 were found to be at increased risk for preterm birth and might have an increased risk of other adverse pregnancy outcomes including higher chances of neonatal morbidity.
3. Most pregnant women infected with Covid-19 will be asymptomatic or have a mild disease, but their health may deteriorate rapidly, which might impact the foetal outcome.
4. It was important that they take all precautions to protect themselves from acquiring Covid-19, including getting vaccinated against Covid-19.
5. The World Health Organization (WHO) recommended vaccination among pregnant women when the benefits of vaccination to the pregnant woman outweigh the potential risks, such as pregnant women at high risk of exposure to Covid-19 and pregnant women with comorbidities that place them in a high-risk group for severe Covid-19 disease.

It was therefore advised that a pregnant woman should take the recommended doses of Covid-19 vaccine.

After the recommendation of NTAGI, discussions were held with professional expert bodies like Indian Medical Association, Indian Academy of Paediatrics, Federation of Obstetric and Gynaecological Societies of India, etc., to refine the operational guidelines for vaccination of pregnant women. Based on these evidence, pregnant women were made eligible for Covid-19 vaccination from 2 July 2021. The inclusion of pregnant and lactating women was a great step to overcome gender-based inequity in access to vaccination.

The country's health system was on a mission mode, delivering the World's largest Covid-19 vaccination programme at the fastest pace. At the same time, researchers were generating evidence on the safety and efficacy of the vaccines in children. Upon review of evidence, NTAGI recommended inclusion of children aged 12–18 years for vaccination. Based on this recommendation and operational feasibility, these children were included in a stepwise manner with adolescents aged 15–18 years from 2 January 2022 and those aged 12–14 years from 16 March 2022.

Around the same time, recommendation for precaution dose was also made, which was started from 10 January 2022, again in a sequential manner, prioritizing elderly with comorbidities followed by all elderly population and ultimately making it available to all citizens aged 18 years and above. The estimated number of each eligible group for Covid-19 vaccination is given at Table 3.1 in Annexure.

The prioritization of population for Covid-19 was an immensely challenging task. Everyone involved in the process had to maintain utmost integrity in the process. With the availability of vaccines being the limiting factor in the initial phase, vaccine eagerness was at an all-time high. The policy makers had to take tough calls to include some groups and to exclude some groups based on some evidence. At such times, they also led by examples. There were quite few policy makers who were medical doctors. However, they did not enrol them as health care workers as they were not directly involved in patient care. They waited for their inclusion based on their age. Such signalling was important to make sure no one felt privileged or entitled to vaccine just based on their place of work. This virtue signalling led to a patient understanding in hundreds of employees and consultants of MoHFW that they waited for their inclusion for vaccination based on their age and were not included as health care workers of front-line workers. Like these, there were many recommendations from various States to include some professional group of workers as Front-Line Workers, but it was all dealt with a scientific acumen and only those demands that were justified were included and rest were not approved.

The prioritization of population for Covid-19 vaccination was an exercise that was done amongst huge pressures but through constant backing of scientific evidence, inclusion of all stakeholders, it provided the streamlining to the world's largest vaccination drive.

3.1 Conclusion

In the face of the unprecedented challenge posed by Covid-19, the global scientific community swiftly rallied to create vaccines against the novel virus. Pioneering efforts from institutions like Pfizer, Moderna, AstraZeneca, and Bharat Biotech yielded remarkable results, with vaccines approved after rigorous trials.

The demand for vaccines surged worldwide, prompting the need for a strategic 'triage' system to optimize distribution. India's response was orchestrated by the

National Expert Group on Vaccine Administration for Covid-19 (NEGVAC), a coalition of experts entrusted with guiding various aspects of the vaccination process. NEGVAC devised strategies for inventory management, vaccine selection, prioritization, financing, and safety. Meanwhile, the established National Technical Advisory Group on Immunization (NTAGI) informed decisions based on evidence, facilitating the introduction of vital vaccines like Hepatitis B, Rotavirus and Inactivated Polio.

The prioritization of vaccine recipients was a complex challenge. NEGVAC's approach was rational, focusing on achieving public health goals: preventing infection, disease, hospitalization, ICU admission, death, and transmission. The rollout began with safeguarding healthcare and front-line workers, acknowledging their critical role in pandemic management. Subsequent phases addressed age and comorbidities, ensuring protection for the most vulnerable segments of society.

Collaborative efforts led to the inclusion of pregnant and lactating women, previously excluded due to limited safety data. Rigorous reviews by experts and medical bodies ensured decisions were rooted in scientific evidence. The process of expansion was gradual, considering both vaccine availability and equitable distribution.

The vaccination drive was an intricate orchestration of policy, science, and operational logistics. It navigated challenges, such as database creation, verification systems, and changing eligibility criteria. With vigilance and integrity, the endeavour aimed at providing equitable access to vaccines while prioritizing those at highest risk.

In summary, India's Covid-19 vaccination journey was marked by scientific rigor, strategic planning, and inclusivity. The collaboration between NEGVAC, NTAGI, and various stakeholders enabled the world's largest vaccination campaign, demonstrating the power of evidence-based decision-making in the face of a global health crisis.

Annexure

Table 3.1 Estimated target population for Covid-19 vaccination

S. no.	State/UT	HCWs	FLWs	12–14 years	15–18 years	18+ years	60+ years
1	A & N Islands	5640	11,090	13,000	23,000	286,000	28,000
2	Andhra Pradesh	498,482	1,618,430	1,490,000	2,441,000	39,522,000	6,557,000
3	Arunachal Pradesh	24,080	78,994	70,000	98,000	1,009,000	100,000
4	Assam	220,900	460,542	1,346,000	2,037,000	23,659,000	2,888,000
5	Bihar	535,673	588,728	5,626,000	8,346,000	73,447,000	9,464,000
6	Chandigarh	26,652	25,856	45,000	72,000	843,000	78,000
7	Chhattisgarh	316,607	334,172	1,046,000	1,635,000	19,651,000	2,586,000
8	Dadra and Nagar Haveli	4967	4894	25,000	34,000	387,000	26,000
9	Daman and Diu	2306	6527	12,000	25,000	340,000	23,000
10	Delhi	267,596	490,180	615,000	1,014,000	15,080,000	1,904,000
11	Goa	25,629	69,417	50,000	74,000	1,166,000	179,000
12	Gujarat	637,112	1,416,092	2,263,000	3,558,000	48,907,000	7,123,000
13	Haryana	257,719	254,775	969,000	1,540,000	20,580,000	2,890,000
14	Himachal Pradesh	94,782	250,455	225,000	352,000	5,523,000	965,000
15	Jammu and Kashmir	108,355	374,181	598,000	833,000	9,409,000	1,268,000
16	Jharkhand	211,641	378,350	1,594,000	2,398,000	24,864,000	3,250,000
17	Karnataka	787,630	1,000,916	2,025,000	3,175,000	48,916,000	7,658,000
18	Kerala	554,131	585,551	1,011,000	1,534,000	26,709,000	5,853,000
19	Ladakh	5663	34,083	9000	13,000	224,000	29,000
20	Lakshadweep	1313	3552	6000	5000	47,000	6000
21	Madhya Pradesh	505,550	584,964	3,044,000	4,800,000	54,949,000	7,161,000
22	Maharashtra	1,324,969	2,243,822	3,919,000	6,063,000	91,435,000	14,548,000
23	Manipur	40,543	124,526	120,000	174,000	2,341,000	315,000

24	Meghalaya	32,623	104,576	144,000	205,000	2,018,000	219,000
25	Mizoram	18,518	41,991	44,000	67,000	867,000	108,000
26	Nagaland	16,810	62,082	94,000	143,000	1,476,000	162,000
27	Odisha	355,481	513,588	1,521,000	2,365,000	32,528,000	5,237,000
28	Puducherry	38,449	24,197	56,000	83,000	1,133,000	155,000
29	Punjab	219,386	1,307,936	865,000	1,419,000	22,738,000	3,829,000
30	Rajasthan	569,133	772,024	2,987,000	4,651,000	51,509,000	6,833,000
31	Sikkim	11,977	17,331	26,000	41,000	517,000	64,000
32	Tamil Nadu	608,907	1,046,929	2,121,000	3,320,000	57,891,000	10,419,000
33	Telangana	320,425	349,718	1,136,000	1,841,000	27,767,000	4,160,000
34	Tripura	54,184	98,527	137,000	213,000	3,163,000	456,000
35	Uttar Pradesh	972,228	1,741,526	8,464,000	14,014,000	147,424,000	18,772,000
36	Uttarakhand	121,173	268,578	392,000	628,000	8,063,000	1,209,000
37	West Bengal	664,361	1,227,935	3,035,000	4,823,000	72,651,000	11,048,000
38	Miscellaneous	94,331	1,534,786				
39	India	10,555,926	20,051,821	47,143,000	74,057,000	939,039,000	137,570,000

Source: MoHFW, Data of HCWs and FLWs was as per the registration on Co-WIN, Age-related estimates were sought from Registrar General of India

Journey from e-VIN to co-WIN and Plan for U-WIN to Track and Digitize the Vaccinations on Real-Time Basis

4

Suhas Dhandore and Abhimanyu Saxena

Abstract

The Covid-19 pandemic led to the development of Co-WIN (Winning over Covid-19), Co-WIN platform, a robust IT system developed by the Ministry of Health and Family Welfare (MoHFW), to manage India's Covid-19 vaccination campaign.

Launched in January 2021, Co-WIN supported the world's largest vaccination program, efficiently managing over 220 crore doses. The platform's success stems from its flexible registration options, ensuring inclusivity for all citizens, its secure and accessible digital vaccination certificates, and its seamless integration with vaccine supply chains and real-time AEFI tracking.

Co-WIN's impact extends beyond India's borders, with over 140 countries participating in the Co-WIN Global Conclave, seeking to replicate its success. The platform's innovative approach has also inspired the development of the U-WIN platform, which extends similar benefits to India's Universal Immunization Programme (UIP), tracking vaccinations for children and pregnant women.

Co-WIN serves as a testament to the transformative power of technology in tackling large-scale public health challenges. Its success underscores the crucial role of robust digital infrastructure in achieving efficient and equitable healthcare delivery.

S. Dhandore (✉)
Airport Health Organisation (APHO), Pune, India
e-mail: suhas.dhandore@nic.in

A. Saxena
Health Systems Strengthening, UNDP, New Delhi, India

M. Agnani et al. (eds.), *India's Covid-19 Vaccine Drive*,
https://doi.org/10.1007/978-981-95-8138-2_4

Keywords

Co-WIN · Vaccination platform · Digital vaccination certificate · IT solution · Scalable platform · Digital health · U-WIN · Technology-driven health solutions

India's Universal Immunization Programme (UIP) is one of the largest public health programs in the world. It targets 30 million pregnant women; 26.7 million newborns annually with 12 million sessions planned each year. There are about 30,000 cold chain points for storing and distributing vaccines. Out of these, 12 antigens, namely, BCG, DPT, OPV, IPV, Measles-Rubella, Hepatitis B, Tetanus, Hib containing Pentavalent vaccine (DPT + HepB+Hib), Pneumococcal Conjugate Vaccine, and Rotavirus vaccine are provided nationwide while Japanese Encephalitis (JE) vaccine has been made available in select endemic districts.

Considering India's population and the large geographic area, vaccines and logistic distribution and its real-time information was a crucial challenge. Further, estimation and forecasting of requirement of vaccines and logistic-related items including such requirements in emergency situations was also a necessity.

Many countries and international organizations were already making considerable investments in the vaccine supply chain to ensure equitable access to vaccines. WHO & UNICEF, in 2009, developed the EVM tool (Effective Vaccine Management), for the assessment of vaccine supply chain and to help countries to ensure and maintain quality of vaccines.

In 2013, the Government of India (GoI) conducted its first national EVM assessment which as expected highlighted the following facts, against the benchmark of 80%:

- Vaccine arrival process was 43%.
- Stock management was 51%.
- Vaccine management process was at 46% &.
- Temperature monitoring was at 54%.

Recognizing that there was an urgent need to make considerable improvements in the supply chain, the Ministry of Health and Family Welfare in 2014 initiated a pilot called eVIN (Electronic Vaccine Intelligence Network) in two districts of Uttar Pradesh (Bareilly and Shajahanpur). The pilot was led by the Immunization Technical Support Unit (ITSU) under Immunization Division. All cold chain handlers were equipped with a basic mobile phone to perform entries related to vaccine stock management and a dashboard was created at the district level.

Later in 2014, under the GAVI Health System Strengthening Support-1 (GAVI-HSS1), the Government of India decided to scale up eVIN in three states and if found successful to another 12 States. The Ministry of Health and Family Welfare further identified United Nation's Development Project (UNDP) for the design, development, implementation, and scale-up of the eVIN solution since UNDP had a strong background in improving health supply chain in more than 70 countries.

In October 2015, UNDP initiated eVIN as a pilot in the three states, i.e., Uttar Pradesh, Madhya Pradesh, and Rajasthan. These states were identified based on immunization coverage and other health indicators. To answer three critical questions—(1) Where are my vaccines? (2) Are they in adequate quantity? (3) Are they stored in recommended temperature?—the 3 Ps model (People, Processes and Product) was applied.

- *People*: Deploying Vaccine and Cold Chain Manager (VCCM) in each district and building capacity of Cold Chain Handlers (CCH).
- *Processes*: Developed standard operating procedures, standard recording, and reporting processes.
- *Product*: An easy-to-use mobile application was developed for cold chain handlers. Another critical component was a SIM-based temperature logger, installed in all refrigerators, that provided real-time data of vaccine storage temperature.

Key Indicators across all vaccine storage points, which were captured are as follows:

1. Stock status of all vaccines
2. Stock out status of all vaccines
3. Excess stock status of all vaccines
4. Vaccine storage temperature
5. Vaccine stock getting expired in next 2 months/3 months

Initial results of eVIN in Uttar Pradesh, Madhya Pradesh, and Rajasthan were very encouraging with more than a 99% adherence rate and significant reduction in stock outs. In 2016, it was decided to expand eVIN to another nine states, i.e., Himachal Pradesh, Gujarat, Bihar, Chhattisgarh, Jharkhand, Odisha, Assam, Manipur, and Nagaland. In 2018, the Government of India did a techno-economic assessment of eVIN, which showed that eVIN saved over 90 million vaccine doses and gave a Return on Investment of 2.91 (every 1 USD invested would return USD 2.91).

The Second National EVM assessment was conducted by UNICEF in 2018. eVIN's impact was clearly visible with improvement in key indicators:

- Vaccine arrival process improved to 60% against 43% in 2013.
- Stock management efficiency improved to 65% against 51% in 2013.
- Vaccine management process rose to 75% against 46% in 2013.
- Temperature monitoring was at 72% against 54% in 2013.

This significant improvement resulted in Ministry of Health & Family Welfare, GoI in reaching to the decision of scaling up eVIN and by December 2020 eVIN was expanded to all 36 states/UTs, digitizing about 30,000 Cold Chain Points

(CCPs) through an efficient web and smartphone-based software application along with the installation of SIM-enabled temperature loggers.

With declaration of Covid-19 pandemic and introduction of clinical trials on Covid-19 vaccine, search was initiated to find and explore suitable IT platform for Covid-19 vaccination in India. There were many concerns being raised for developing a suitable, robust platform which captured the required essentials of all adult populations in time along with generation of digital vaccine certificate for every dose and every beneficiary vaccinated. Experts had an argument that Universal Immunization Programme (UIP) so far has captured only limited cohort of children and pregnant women requiring vaccination. It does not give details regarding beneficiaries who have been immunized, does not talk about the time, place, and healthcare provider who have vaccinated, and therefore is unable to generate routine vaccination certificate containing all the aforementioned details. The remaining work in comparison to what is currently available is huge in nature and looking to urgency and time constraint, it was opined that creating a fresh digital platform would offer a better solution than doing a patchwork on existing IT platform.

A series of meetings and deliberations were held at various levels to decide on data capturing for Covid-19 vaccination and MoHFW officials getting convinced with the advantages of building it further on eVIN had to defend their case. The Immunization division forwarded the basic premise that eVIN has matured to the present state due to tremendous efforts in terms of both money and time and further, States/UTs now have a trained cadre of human resources to manage this on-line platform. Given the pressing need to roll out the Covid-19 vaccine urgently, creating a beneficiary module on current system will save not only resources but also be beneficial in terms of time.

Taking into the considerations the aforementioned facts, a decision was taken to build new IT platform with beneficiary module for Covid-19 vaccination which would have linkages with eVIN platform so that Covid-19 vaccine administration data is be captured through new IT platform while vaccine consumption data would get captured in eVIN platform, so that both the data parameters can be linked together.

Since eVIN was developed by UNDP, the development partner of Immunization, Program the same agency was entrusted to design and develop a new IT platform for Covid-19 vaccination to be titled as Co-VIN, i.e., Covid-19 Vaccination Intelligence Network. But after due deliberation meetings, the name was finally decided to be Co-WIN, i.e., Wining over Covid-19.

A core group was set up under the Chairpersonship of the Joint Secretary (eHealth) with all relevant stakeholders like the development team, UNDP, Immunization Division, Centre for Health Informatics (CHI), eHealth Division, Covid-19 War Room Team, NIC, and IIT Delhi to discuss and deliberate on designing and development of the IT Platform. Daily 9:00 AM meetings were held with various stakeholders to assign time-bound tasks and review the progress along with timelines.

On regular intervals, the progress related to Co-WIN was shared, which yielded the desired outcomes. The first Dry Run of Co-WIN application was conducted on December 28 and 29, 2020, in two districts each in four states, i.e., Gujarat, Andhra Pradesh, Punjab, and Assam. Second Dry Run of Co-WIN application was conducted after 3 days on January 2, 2021, across all 36 states/UTs. It was conducted in 125 districts and 285 Session sites across the country.

- These dry runs were aimed to comprehensively test the entire Covid-19 vaccination process in an end to end manner and included the following:
- Planning and preparation in line with the Operational Guidelines.
- Setting up facilities and user profiles on the Co-WIN application.
- Establishing and mapping vaccination sites.
- Uploading healthcare workers (HCW) beneficiary data on Co-WIN.
- Planning sessions and deploying vaccinators.
- Mobilizing teams.
- Managing vaccine and logistics at session sites.
- Receiving vaccines at the district level and allocating them using Co-WIN.
- Simulating beneficiary vaccination and reporting.
- Conducting review meetings at block, district, and state levels to provide feedback for further action.

Primary objectives of these dry runs were as follows:

- Evaluate the practicality of using the Co-WIN application in real-world conditions.
- Test the coordination between planning, execution, and reporting mechanisms.
- Identify challenges and provide solutions before actual implementation.
- Build confidence among program managers at all levels.

These successful dry runs enabled the health system to identify gaps and issues in the process of Covid-19 vaccination including various end-to-end processes on Co-WIN platform, i.e., registration of beneficiary, appointment scheduling, session planning, verification of beneficiary using prescribed Photo ID Card, vaccination of beneficiary, certificate generation, and Adverse Effects Following Immunization (AEFI) reporting. Based on the suggestions and feedback received necessary changes were made on Co-WIN platform. Conducting the dry runs helped a lot in finalizing the functionality of each module of Co-WIN Platform.

Extensive trainings to Health workers to utilize Co-WIN platform was ensured through preparation of Video modules, which explained the functionality of the application in simple and comprehensible manner. This training was ensured to the last mile across all the States/UTs through virtual mode. Further, at the backdrop of continuous amendments of national Covid-19 vaccination policy, it was imperative to do modification on Co-WIN and impart the skills to grassroot-level workers. No physical trainings were conducted at national/state/district/block level due to the ongoing Covid-19 pandemic all trainings were conducted in virtual mode.

As soon as any functionality in Co-WIN was ready, voice over videos were prepared for respective module and after review and testing of same, and were released for circulation, through different WhatsApp groups from national to state and from state to district as well as from district to field-level workers.

Looking to the importance of Co-WIN for National Covid-19 Vaccination Program and to ensure inter departmental coordination and for building confidence in the system, on the lines of creating empowered groups on various issues related to Covid-19 pandemic, an Empowered Group on Covid-19 Vaccine Administration (EGVAC) was also created on January 8, 2021, under the Chairmanship of Dr. R.S Sharma, Chief Executive Officer, National Health Authority (NHA) & Ex-Chairperson, TRAI with other members including Secretary, MeitY, Secretary, D/o Health & Family Welfare, CEO-UIDAI, Additional Secretary in charge of National Covid-19 Vaccination Program, DoHFW (as convener), Adviser (IT), UIDAI, CEO-NeGD, Joint Secretary DOHFW and Director PMO.

EGVAC was mandated to take all necessary measures and decisions for effective implementation of Co-WIN platform for successful implementation of Covid-19 vaccination program.

With this preparation, the world's largest Covid-19 Vaccination Drive was launched on January 16, 2021, by Hon'ble Prime Minister of India. Considering ongoing Covid-19 pandemic at the backdrop of rising cases and deaths in the country, the launch of Covid-19 vaccination and Co-WIN Platform was held in virtual mode with webcasting of entire events across the country.

The Co-WIN system facilitated the creation of various user roles (admins, supervisors, vaccinators), registration of beneficiaries, facilities/planning units, and session sites. It also enabled the planning, scheduling, and implementation of vaccination sessions. By the end of February 2021, over 1.23 crore doses (approximately 1.09 crore first doses and around 14 lakh second doses) had been administered across more than 2,63,000 sessions at over 45,000 sites, primarily targeting healthcare workers and frontline workers.

Following the guidance of NEGVAC, the next phase of vaccination began on March 1, 2021, targeting citizens above 60 years of age and those aged 45–60 years with comorbidities. This led to the development of Co-WIN 2.0 by the Ministry of Health and Family Welfare (MoHFW) to simplify the registration process based on feedback from Phase 1 of the vaccination drive.

A guidance note was issued outlining the principles for vaccination of eligible citizens and defining roles, responsibilities, and standard operating procedures (SOPs) for various modules of Co-WIN 2.0. This included key features intended for use by program managers at the state/district and facility levels.

A "Vaccination Cycle" of not more than 28 days was introduced for planning the target number of doses by the state/UT governments. Targets for the doses to be added for each Vaccination Cycle were set at the district level, and within each district, at the individual vaccination center level. This information was used to prepare and enter vaccination timetables into Co-WIN, detailing various types of vaccination slots for each center.

Each vaccination center had slots for reserved and open appointments. Reserved slots included mobilization slots for on-site registration, verification, and vaccination on the same day, as well as slots for the second dose for beneficiaries who had received their first dose. Open slots were for online appointments by the general public. The number of open slots for a session was determined by subtracting the number of reserved slots from the center's session capacity.

The Framework and underlying Principles followed for Co-WIN 2.0 were based on determination of target number of doses for a vaccination cycle and included the following:

(a) The vaccination schedule was closely linked to the availability of vaccine doses. States/UTs decided the target number of doses for a vaccination cycle based on the available doses and expected additional doses.
(b) When a beneficiary received the first dose, Co-WIN automatically confirmed the appointment for the second dose at the same vaccination center.
(c) The Ministry periodically indicated the state-level allocation of vaccine doses.

A Covid-19 vaccination Center was mandatorily required to be a health facility and were of following two types:

(a) Government Covid-19 Vaccination Center (GCVC)—These facilities encompassed all Government Medical Colleges, District Hospitals, Sub-District Hospitals, Community Health Centers, Primary Health Centers, and Sub-Health Centers. Additionally, these also included Central Institutions, health facilities from other Ministries such as Railways, ESIC, and Home, and all CGHS Dispensaries.
(b) Private Covid-19 Vaccination Center (PCVC)—For a private health facility to be designated as a Private Covid-19 Vaccination Center (PCVC), it needed to be empaneled under the Ayushman Bharat-Pradhan Mantri Jan Arogya Yojana (AB-PMJAY), the Central Government Health Scheme (CGHS), or any health insurance scheme of the state/UT government. Additionally, the facility had to meet the following criteria:
    1. Adequate cold chain equipment and capacity
    2. Sufficient space for designated waiting area, vaccination, and post vaccination observation
    3. Trained vaccinators and verifiers
    4. Capacity to manage the Adverse Events Following Immunization (AEFI), in accordance with the prescribed norms and guidelines

Although the list of Covid-19 Vaccination Centers (CVCs) with available slots were accessible to the public through Co-WIN or other Co-WIN compliant applications, however state/UT governments were advised to widely publicize this list through all available channels to inform citizens. District administrators were responsible for creating a vaccination timetable (using Co-WIN 2.0) for each CVC based on the target doses and planned coverage duration, as decided by the respective state/UT government. The minimum daily capacity was set to equal the number of second doses due at a CVC that day.

In addition to the CVC capacity, district administrators were required to specify the percentage of remaining capacity (CVC Capacity—second dose reserve) to be opened for online appointments. If this percentage was zero, the session was entirely for reserved slots and not visible for online appointment. Conversely, if the specified percentage was 100%, there were no mobilization slots, and all remaining capacity was classified as open slots available for online appointments.

Access to citizens was granted through several routes. These included provisions of (a) advance self-registration, (b) facilitated cohort registration, and (c) on-site registration. The details of these provisions are as follows:

(a) Self-Registration (Online Registration and Appointment Scheduling):
   1. Citizens could register and schedule appointments through the Co-WIN portal or other IT applications like Arogya Setu.
   2. During registration, citizens provided basic demographic details and details of the prescribed photo ID card for verification at the vaccination site.
   3. The Co-WIN portal displayed a list of CVCs with available slots, allowing citizens to choose their preferred center and book an appointment based on the available slots.

(b) Facilitated Cohort Registration (Mobilization of Beneficiaries): States/UTs were encouraged to reserve certain sessions at CVCs for on-site registration. In such cases, state/UT/district teams would undertake the required efforts and ensure necessary arrangements to mobilize enough citizens, to fully utilize the planned capacity.

(c) On-Site Registration (Walk-In Appointments): Eligible citizens could also register on-site for vaccination to prevent overcrowding and accommodate willing beneficiaries.

All citizens, whether they registered online or through on-site registration, were advised to carry one of the following Government-generated IDs for verification at the vaccination site:

- ADHAAR Card
- Driving License
- PAN Card
- Passport
- Pension Passbook
- NPR Smart Card
- Voter ID (EPIC)
- Unique Disability Identification Card (UDID)
- Ration Card with Photo
- Student Photo ID card

All verifiers and vaccinators designated for a session had access to the full list of citizens to be vaccinated, as available in Co-WIN. All vaccination events were recorded in real time through the Co-WIN vaccinator module.

The various modules available on Co-WIN were as follows:

1. Beneficiary Registration & Appointment Scheduling Module—It was used for online (self) registration or on-site (walk-in) registration of beneficiary and for taking online appointment for vaccination at desired vaccination center as per vaccine availability and eligibility criteria. The beneficiary would be able to download appointment slip after successful booking of appointment for vaccination. There was also a provision to reschedule appointment already scheduled for desired date and desired vaccination center as per the convenience of beneficiary. The beneficiary could also delete his/her registration only if not vaccinated with any single dose.
2. Session Creation Module—Through this module, vaccination sessions were created at Covid-19 vaccination centers (CVCs) by district administrator in case of Government CVC and by session site manager of private CVC. Vaccination session was created for each vaccine type at designated Covid-19 vaccination center depending upon age group, type of dose (first, second, or precaution dose), mode of beneficiary registration (online/onsite) etc.
3. Beneficiary Verification Module—It was used for verification of beneficiary using one of the prescribed photo ID cards prior to vaccination. Photo ID card type, Photo ID number, and scanned copy of ID card were uploaded on Co-WIN during verification process. If beneficiary have provided Aadhaar number, then there was provision to do Aadhaar authentication and to generate Ayushyman Bharat Account Number (ABHA ID) with consent of beneficiary. Three modes were used for Aadhaar authentication of beneficiary—demographic authentication, biometric authentication, OTP-based authentication.
4. Vaccination Module—This module was used by vaccinator to conduct vaccination of beneficiary and to record vaccination dose on Co-WIN. There was specific time interval in between first and second dose and in between second and precaution dose depending upon type of beneficiary, type of vaccine, and special dispensation in case of international traveler.
5. Certificate Generation Module—This module was used for generation of digital vaccination certificate after updating vaccination dose of beneficiary on Co-WIN.
6. AEFI Reporting Module—After vaccine administration, if beneficiary reported adverse events following immunization (AEFI) of any kind, such event can be reported through this module.

Text SMSs were sent to beneficiaries to register mobile numbers on following occasions:

- At the time of registration
- Thereafter at each login (OTP)
- After successful booking of online appointment
- After each vaccination dose updation
- Due dose reminders—3 days before due date, on due date, thereafter every third day for 4 times (total 6 reminders each for second dose and precaution dose)

The feature of search your nearest vaccination Center utility was available on Co-WIN homepage to get a preview list of the nearest vaccination centers and check availability of vaccination slots for beneficiaries based on district location, PIN, and map.

Co-WIN contributed significantly to ensuring equitable and inclusive vaccination across multilingual states, with multiple registration modes which for enhanced accessibility. It also facilitated unbiased vaccine distribution by serving as the single source of truth for vaccination related data. Its dynamic architecture could adapt to changing circumstances. Timely information on vaccination and adverse events following immunization (AEFI) from Co-WIN aided NTAGI and MoHFW in policy analysis and corrections.

Co-WIN was an all-inclusive platform for vaccination of all kinds of eligible beneficiaries. Even the beneficiary does not have mobile number and or prescribed photo ID card, such PWI (People without Identity cards), beneficiaries got vaccinated in special sessions which were conducted on the direction of District Task Force (DTF).

CO-WIN provided the following advantages to the citizens

- Inclusive: Co-WIN ensured universal access to vaccination, overcoming physical, linguistic, digital, and socio-economic barriers.
- Convenient and Transparent: It provided easy access to information on vaccination sessions and centers, allowing online booking of appointments at the preferred center.
- Flexible: Citizens could register online or on-site, offering flexibility in the vaccination process.
- Anytime anywhere vaccination: Co-WIN allowed registration at any convenient access point, ensuring services in areas with limited internet and mobile connectivity.
- Informative: It tracked the time interval between vaccine doses and provided alerts for the second dose.
- Digitally verifiable: Co-WIN issued digital certificates after each dose, which could be verified online and offline.
- Provisions for vulnerable groups: Special vaccination sessions were arranged for people without a valid photo ID proof.

The following advantages of Co-WIN were for Program Managers:

- Scalable supply chain management: Ability to manage large transaction loads administering over 10 million doses multiple times per day. It holistically managed vaccine supply chain planning and operations in government and private setups.
- Optimized vaccination session management: Efficiently and effectively managed vaccination sessions for both online and on-site modes, including publishing information on doses and timings.

- Coverage tracking and reporting: Monitored vaccination progress at a granular level, capturing geographic and demographic coverage and providing reports and dashboards.
- User-friendly interface: Co-WIN provided easy-to-use interfaces for all system users, especially front-end vaccinators.
- Minimized vaccine wastage: Assessed the vaccine wastage and facilitated measures to minimize it.
- AEFI tracking: Provisioned for reporting of AEFI in real-time basis for investigation and intervention, as needed.
- Data Aggregation: Collated vaccination data to support research and development, including for newer vaccines and booster doses, and to inform pandemic planning and policy decisions at various levels.

The Co-WIN application has been a cornerstone of India's Covid-19 vaccination program, serving as a comprehensive cloud-based IT solution for planning, implementing, and monitoring vaccinations. It provided end-to-end solutions down to the vaccinator level and acted as the digital backbone of the program. Co-WIN was scalable, inclusive, and had a dual interface for citizens and administrators.

The system tracked beneficiaries and vaccines in real time at the national, state, district, and sub-district levels, enabling monitoring of utilization, wastage, and coverage. Co-WIN facilitated various roles for managing the vaccination drive, including user creation, beneficiary registration, appointment scheduling, and session planning.

It was accessible in 12 regional languages and offered several user-friendly features. Online registration and booking were not mandatory, as Co-WIN supported on-site registration and vaccination for individuals and groups, especially for those without internet access. Assisted registration through Common Service Centers (CSCs) and the 1075 helpline was also available.

Online registration and booking an appointment in advance were not mandatory to receive vaccination services. Co-WIN provided additional registration and vaccination options, including on-site or walk-in registration and vaccination for individuals and groups, especially for those without internet access or smartphones. Registration assistance was available through Common Service Centers (CSCs) and the 1075 helpline. Special vaccination sessions were organized for individuals without specified identity cards. Near-to-home vaccination sessions were arranged for the elderly and persons with disabilities, where all vaccinations were conducted through on-site registrations. Co-WIN also offered features to reserve vaccination slots for the second dose, ensuring timely administration after the first dose.

Indian Covid-19 vaccination certificates are standardized and conform to the evolving WHO guidance on verifiable vaccination certificates and compliant with WHO-DDCC: VS data dictionary. India released format and design of vaccination certificate for international travelers with incorporation of all relevant parameters as per WHO guidelines. The Co-WIN vaccination certificate included a digitally signed and secure QR code.

The vaccination certificate can be verified online using a third-party verification app or the verification utility on the Co-WIN portal at https://verify.cowin.gov.in/. Upon successful verification, the screen displays a message stating "Certificate Successfully Verified," along with details such as name, age, gender, certificate ID, beneficiary ID, vaccine name, date of dose, and vaccination status. In cases where the certificate is not genuine, the screen shows the message "Certificate Invalid." This verification utility is commonly used at points of entry, such as airports, to confirm vaccination status.

In view of helping beneficiary in context to generate corrected certificate by addition/editing content on certificate various utilities were provided on Co-WIN portal for applying self-correction of vaccination certificate:

- Updation in Vaccination Certificate—Changes were provisioned regarding Name/Age/Gender/Photo ID of a beneficiary, if there were any data entry errors during registration.
- Merge Two Dose #1 Certificate—If a beneficiary has multiple provisional certificates for Dose #1 generated through different accounts, they can be merged to generate a final vaccination certificate.
- Addition of Passport Details to Vaccination Certificate—This is done to link vaccination certificate with passport number for international travel. Beneficiaries who have received two doses of Covid-19 vaccine could update existing photo identity to passport number and date of birth to avail an international vaccination certificate.
- Report Unknown Member Registered with Co-WIN Account—In case an unknown member was added to account, utility could be used to remove that member from the account.
- Transfer a Member to New Mobile Number—In case beneficiary wanted to transfer a member from present account to another account with new mobile number.
- Regenerate Final Certificate—If vaccination date or batch number was not same as in final certificate, error could be corrected by regenerating the certificate.
- Vaccination Date Correction—To correct the vaccine date in vaccination certificate, application could be submitted for approval through District Immunization Officer (DIO).
- Revoke Vaccination—To revoke vaccination status from vaccination certificate from precaution dose to fully vaccinated, from fully vaccinated to partially vaccinated, and from partially vaccinated to no vaccinated.

The Union Cabinet had approved proposal on bilateral agreement on mutual recognition of Covid-19 vaccination certificates with willing countries and delegated the authority to a committee comprising External Affairs Minister and Minister for Health & Family Welfare. Indian Covid-19 vaccination certificates are verifiable in online mode.

A Task Force was constituted by MoHFW, with representation from Ministry of Civil Aviation (MoCA), Ministry of External Affairs (MEA), Department of Health

Research (DHR-ICMR), National Health Authority (NHA) & Ministry of Health & Family Welfare (MoHFW), for co-ordination and information exchange and collation of the requirements for travel documents (RT-PCR test reports and Covid-19 vaccination certificates) acceptable to various countries for international travel.

Co-WIN supported multi-distribution methods (digitally available on smartphones and printable for non-smartphone users) multilingual (17 languages) vaccination certificate templates and API-based integration with travel wallets/passes and other health systems.

The Government of India agreed to join the WHO Covid-19 Technology Access Pool initiative. Co-WIN, which is an inclusive, scalable, secure platform, was offered for replication in the other countries along with necessary technical assistance as per the agreed terms and condition.

National Health Authority (NHA) was designated as the authorized agency for signing the MOU on behalf of the MoHFW, GoI, with the interested countries under the Co-WIN Global Outreach Programme.

On July 5, 2021, the Government of India organized Co-WIN global conclave with an aim of sharing experiences, expertise, and resources of the country with the global community in the battle against Covid-19 in which around 141 countries participated with many countries expressing interest in adopting this versatile platform to orchestrate vaccination in their countries, including Guyana, Malavi, Vietnam, Sierra Leone, Fiji, and Nepal.

After the stupendous success of Co-WIN platform, based on the learnings and experience, new dedicated IT platform namely U-WIN was designed and developed by MoHFW to record every vaccination event under Universal Immunization Programme (UIP), i.e., for vaccination of pregnant women and for children of 0–5 years. Soft launch of pilot phase of U-WIN Platform was done in 65 identified districts in 36 states/UTs on January 11, 2023, and at present, it is in the phase of national scale up.

4.1 Conclusion

India's Universal Immunization Programme (UIP) is a mammoth public health initiative targeting millions of pregnant women and newborns annually. However, effective vaccine distribution across India's vast and diverse landscape posed significant challenges. In response, the Government of India initiated the Electronic Vaccine Intelligence Network (eVIN) pilot in 2014. eVIN leveraged technology and strategic interventions to improve vaccine supply chains, resulting in remarkable achievements.

The eVIN approach encompassed the 3 Ps model—People, Processes, and Product—to address vaccine distribution challenges comprehensively. It deployed Vaccine and Cold Chain Manager (VCCMs) and equipped Cold Chain Handlers (CCHs) with a user-friendly mobile app. Standard operating procedures, real-time monitoring of vaccine storage temperatures, and other innovations were introduced, boosting accountability and transparency in the supply chain.

The initial results were impressive, with adherence rates exceeding 99% and substantial reductions in stockouts. The success prompted the expansion of eVIN leading to significant improvements across key indicators, including vaccine arrival, stock management, vaccine management, and temperature monitoring.

A techno-economic assessment in 2018 demonstrated eVIN's incredible impact, saving over 90 million vaccine doses and yielding a remarkable Return on Investment (ROI) of 2.91. With its proven efficacy and tangible benefits, eVIN was scaled up nationwide. By December 2020, it had digitized around 30,000 Cold Chain Points (CCPs) across all 36 states/union territories, revolutionizing India's vaccine distribution system.

The eVIN success story serves as an inspiring example of how innovative technology, strategic planning, and collaboration can overcome complex challenges, ensuring equitable access to lifesaving vaccines for millions of children and securing their brighter future.

The government's decision to create a new IT platform for Covid-19 vaccination stemmed from the need to capture and manage essential data efficiently, given the urgency of the situation. This new platform was built with a beneficiary module that linked to the existing eVIN platform, enabling comprehensive data tracking.

The Co-WIN platform underwent thorough testing through multiple dry runs aimed to assess operational feasibility, test linkages between different processes, identify challenges, and build confidence in the system.

Extensive training was conducted using video modules to educate healthcare workers and other stakeholders on the functionality of the Co-WIN platform.

The Co-WIN platform allowed for user creation, beneficiary registration, facility planning, and session scheduling. The launch of the world's largest Covid-19 vaccination drive occurred virtually, given the pandemic's ongoing nature.

With the need to expand vaccination to other age groups, Co-WIN 2.0 was introduced, simplifying the registration and scheduling process. The platform incorporated principles for determining the target number of doses for each vaccination cycle, ensuring efficient vaccine distribution and administration.

Multiple pathways were established for citizen access, including advance self-registration, facilitated cohort registration, and on-site registration. The Co-WIN platform provided modules for beneficiary registration, session creation, verification, vaccination, certificate generation, and adverse event reporting.

Co-WIN, a groundbreaking cloud-based IT solution, has played a pivotal role in India's Covid-19 vaccination drive. This comprehensive platform ensured equitable and inclusive vaccination across multilingual states while offering multiple registration modes to ensure accessibility for all citizens. It served as a single source of truth for vaccination-related data, promoting unbiased distribution of vaccines, and supporting policy analysis and correction. Co-WIN's dynamic architecture allowed it to evolve with changing circumstances, contributing to efficient management and data-driven decision-making.

Co-WIN's role extended beyond Covid-19, as it also managed other vaccine programs. The platform's flexibility, inclusivity, and dual interface (citizen and administrator) made it an integral part of India's vaccination strategy. Co-WIN's real-time tracking capabilities helped monitor beneficiaries and vaccines at various levels, ensuring optimal utilization and coverage.

Notably, Co-WIN provided tools for correcting and verifying vaccination certificates, complying with international standards for travel. This flexibility and versatility led to interest from other countries, with over 140 nations participating in the Co-WIN Global Conclave to explore adoption.

Building on Co-WIN's success, the development of U-WIN expanded its capabilities to record vaccination events under the Universal Immunization Programme, benefiting pregnant women and children. The system's phased national rollout showcases the ongoing innovation and adaptability of India's vaccination management platforms.

In conclusion, Co-WIN's impact on India's vaccination campaign has been transformative, ensuring inclusivity, transparency, and effective management through its dynamic architecture and versatile features.

Communication Plan for National Covid-19 Vaccination Program

5

Veena Dhawan and Nishant Shukla

Abstract

This chapter delves into the communication strategy and planning for the Covid-19 vaccination drive for the country. The strategy aimed to provide timely, accurate information in a transparent manner. This approach aimed to dispel vaccine-related apprehensions, foster acceptance, and encourage widespread uptake. This chapter offers insights into use of traditional media and effectively leveraging new age digital platforms to address misinformation, public anxiety, vaccine eagerness, and vaccine hesitancy.

In addition to discussing the innovative use of popular public programs like the Prime Minister's *Mann Ki Baat*, this chapter outlines the collaborative communication efforts between the Ministry of Health and 22 other central ministries. It also sheds light on lessons learned in crisis communication through the establishment of a well-designed National Media Rapid Response Cell. This initiative played a critical role in combating the "infodemic" and addressing the spread of fake news during the pandemic.

Keywords

Public health communication · Public health crisis · Behavior change · Misinformation · Infodemic · Jan Andolan · Covid-19 appropriate behavior (CAB) · Vaccine eagerness · Vaccine hesitancy

---

V. Dhawan (✉) · N. Shukla
MoHFW, New Delhi, India

M. Agnani et al. (eds.), *India's Covid-19 Vaccine Drive*,
https://doi.org/10.1007/978-981-95-8138-2_5

Health communication has a critical role in all public health intervention due to Information Asymmetry among the citizens. It educates and raises awareness about health issues, encourages behavior change, and mitigates risks. It serves as a powerful tool to empower individuals to make informed decisions about their health and foster healthier habits. Effective communication is critically important during such public health emergencies like Covid-19, for perceptions of risks, provide guidance, and prevent panic. By promoting social norms and peer influence, health communication can debunk misinformation and ensure the accurate dissemination of information. Overall, health communication is a key player in public health that enables collaboration, informed decision-making, and the creation of healthier societies.

Good communication helps people address their fears with concrete information they can use.[1] This was demonstrated well throughout the Covid-19 vaccination program management. The communication strategy for worlds' largest vaccination drive was framed to support the Covid-19 vaccines rollout in India to disseminate timely, accurate, and transparent information about the vaccine(s) to alleviate apprehensions about the vaccine, ensure its acceptance, and encourage uptake. Right from the beginning to the announcement of the end of pandemic, it was a two-way communication process, which was not something made in silos by policymakers but was framed through active participation of community at large. Using the social influence or endorsements from experts and official voices, the communication strategy involved all credible source of information to connect with the masses, as there were legitimate concerns about the pandemic in general and introduction of a new vaccine in particular, which required evidence-based answers to get citizen's acceptance and building confidence.

As early as on October 8, 2020, India launched a mass movement "Jan Aandolan" for Covid-19 appropriate behavior. The low-cost high intensity campaign to intensify this "Jan Aandolan" focused on "Wearing Mask, Following Physical Distancing, and Maintaining Hand Hygiene."[2]

Engaging communication campaigns were the cornerstone of India's fight against the Covid-19 pandemic and its execution of the world's largest vaccination drive. Leveraging the widespread access people had to news via smartphone, digital platform and 24/7 multilingual broadcast, the government transformed the vaccine drive into a participatory moment. This two-way communication was key to reach the country's vaccination targets and overcoming public health communication challenges.

The Covid-19 pandemic required to address public's anxiety about a new deadly virus engulfing the entire world through various strategies including by communicating to citizens on evolving polices about Covid-19 containment, travel restrictions, Covid-19 appropriate behavior (CAB), vaccine eagerness, and vaccine hesitancy. The age of digital communication especially with high smartphone penetration and affordable internet services has led to higher use of social media platforms such as Twitter and WhatsApp. This also translated into the spread of

[1] https://ccp.jhu.edu/2020/03/17/communicating-about-coronavirus/.

[2] https://pib.gov.in/PressReleaseIframePage.aspx?PRID=1662449.

misinformation and myths regarding Covid-19 vaccination, which had the potential to adversely impact the vaccination drive. This phenomenon of the rapid spread of misinformation has been defined as an "infodemic" by the World Health Organization. In order to tackle this, the strategy was to address such misinformation in a timely and factual manner across all traditional and digital platforms.

Right from the beginning, the vaccine program managers were made aware of all the developments, and therefore they timely planned a regular communication with public on all aspects related to Covid-19 vaccination.

The communication efforts with the citizens continued on a regular basis. A consistent and clear communication was made with scientists, frontline workers, doctors, healthcare workers, and public at large. People were eager to listen to PM's Mann Ki Baat radio program, which was very well summed up by Governor of Madhya Pradesh Shri Mangubhai Patel. "PM Modi's 'Mann ki Baat' has enabled India and the people in fighting against the covid-19 pandemic and the vaccination drives against the viral infection."[3]

Most Indians have grown hearing the powerful words—Do bond zindagi ki in the voice of legendry actor Amitabh Bachchan against the Polio virus. This effective campaign is a success story in public health space and was instrumental in making polio campaign a household name in India. With the experience of running mass campaigns for Polio, it was clear that a strong communication strategy must be in place with all information for citizens to take an informed choice.

The Covid-19 vaccination was provided free to all citizens and was voluntary, so it was even more critical that the citizens had the right and real-time information about vaccines and vaccination campaign. It was important to share clear, accurate, and transparent information to build vaccine confidence in the community.

A clear governance mechanism was put in place so that timely and clear information is sent on regular basis to the States/district administration through the State and district task forces and through them to the program managers and the frontline health workers. The messages were crisp and clear to avoid any ambiguity. There was a clear line of command that could reiterate these messages to those seeking clarification. The same structure was used to gathering back updates on the program from the States and districts. The 360-degree Covid-19 communication strategy focused on four key areas:

1. Information on the New Covid-19 Vaccine: To provide prompt, simple information on the Covid-19 vaccine(s) and vaccination processes.
2. Vaccine Eagerness: Pandemic had affected everyone's life and therefore they all were eager to be back to their routine with vaccination being perceived to be "the intervention." But being a biological product, it needed time to be manufactured and therefore for health system, prioritization was important to cover those first who were more vulnerable and at risk of developing serious disease. So, it was

[3] https://www.outlookindia.com/national/pm-modi-s-mann-ki-baat-helped-india-to-fight-against-covid-19-mp-governor-mangubhai-patel-news-282496.

critical to ensure understanding and acceptance of the phased and prioritized approach to overcome concerns of the population waiting for vaccination.

3. Vaccine Hesitancy: Build and maintain public confidence on the safety and efficacy of the new vaccines used in the program and hence improve acceptability.
4. Covid-19 Appropriate Behaviors (CAB): Maintain and sustain key preventive behaviors, i.e., wearing masks, maintaining physical distance and hand washing with soap before, during and after vaccination. Covid-19 appropriate behavior (CAB) was to be followed not just during and after vaccination but even otherwise.

Communication strategy served as a key guidance to the state program managers, IEC officials and partners to plan and effectively implement the strategic approach to address the vaccine eagerness, vaccine hesitancy, and for maintenance of the Covid-19 appropriate behavior. The strategy was well complemented with IEC materials prepared with simple yet effective messages for use by states at grassroots level. These materials were customized by states and union territories to be put up at the vaccination centers. The posters/banners prepared had clear instructions about the vaccines and the vaccination process.

Traditional media platforms including the radio platforms like FM channels and Community radios played a key role to educate, inform, and address myths and misinformation around Covid-19 vaccination.

There were several reports[4] about low uptake of Covid-19 vaccines in the early phase of the launch of program. These were largely related to Covaxin as the protocols for vaccination required consent of the citizen. This type of unique vaccine hesitancy was effectively countered by no less person than the Prime minister himself, who got vaccinated with Covaxin to clarify the doubts about its safety, immunogenicity, and efficacy.

Further, the Health Ministry collaborated effectively with the Ministry of Tribal Affairs to address the issue of low vaccine uptake in tribal districts of the country.[5] Both the ministries worked together and developed communication outreach with the Tribal Cooperative Marketing Development Federation (TRIFED). TRIFED involved local faith leaders and community elders to bust myths and misconceptions around vaccines. Multiple community awareness programs were held at fertilizers outlet centers, haats and bazaars, milk collection points, and Van Dhan Vikas Kendras.

Chaired by the Secretary of Ministry of Information and Broadcasting, the Empowered Group enabled the Ministry of Health and Family Welfare, Government of India, to engage with 22 Central Ministries, such as Ministry of Rural Development and Ministry of Panchayati Raj among others. By activating their extensive field network, the government ensured the widespread dissemination of Factual information and positive reinforcement regarding the vaccine drive.

[4] https://pubmed.ncbi.nlm.nih.gov/37039201/.

[5] https://www.deccanherald.com/national/centre-launches-covid-19-vaccination-campaign-for-tribals-1008983.html.

As the vaccine was new, rumors related to vaccine and vaccination process was anticipated. For example, there were media posts expressing concerns regarding infertility among population of reproductive age after vaccination;[6] multiple side effects of Covid-19 vaccines;[7] an increase in the cases of severe AEFI which have also resulted in "succumbing of patients" post vaccination among others.[8]

The program was already prepared to address such false and misleading information which created a situation of infodemic, in digital and physical environments creating confusion and adopting risk-taking behaviors, that could harm to health. Such infodemic also leads to mistrust in health authorities and undermined the public health response. Further, such infodemics may intensify or lengthen outbreaks when people are unsure about mechanisms to protect their health and the health of people around them. Then, with growing digitization—an expansion of social media and internet use—unverified/fake information can spread more rapidly. This can help to fill information voids more quickly but can also amplify harmful messages.[9]

To address this infodemic and not let it impact the ambitious Covid-19 vaccination program, a National Media Rapid Response cell, which was set up at the ministry to regularly scan the traditional media and social media platforms for any misinformation related to Covid-19 pandemic and vaccination and for taking timely action, played an important role. This cell daily shared the information that was getting circulated with details of it and each of such news/article/message was investigated by the immunization division for timely rebuttals, if needed. However, there were miscreant groups that were trying to gain ground by negative publicity around the campaign were strategically ignored.

A fact check unit in Press Information Bureau under the Ministry of Information and Broadcasting was constituted to effectively curb misinformation on various Covid-19-related issues including vaccination and report fake and unscientific health-related news. It was also ensured that fact check videos by key health experts were prepared and disseminated across all traditional and digital media platforms to provide correct information for public.

Traditional media approach of media briefing (PIB Media briefings on Covid-19 can be accessed through YouTube) was the most watched and most discussed telecast at that time that informed about the status of vaccine availability and vaccination and latest in research in a transparent and comprehensive manner to the media and through them to the masses. However, it needed quick, regular, and timely engagement with media without fail. As a first step, capacity building of media spokespersons, radio jockeys, radio program heads, and social media influencers with a diverse outreach was carried out. This enabled these key influencers to be equipped with facts and scientific rationale. They had access to the ministry spokespersons to quickly verify any fake news or misinformation and correct it on their respective channels. This enabled in further amplifying dissemination of right

---

[6] https://pib.gov.in/PressReleasePage.aspx?PRID=1731436.

[7] https://pib.gov.in/PressReleaseIframePage.aspx?PRID=1891777.

[8] https://pib.gov.in/PressReleasePage.aspx?PRID=1727196.

[9] https://www.who.int/health-topics/infodemic#tab=tab_1.

information on the vaccination drive, ally public's fears, and counter misconceptions. There were regular shows like "Aarogya Bharat," where the experts were updating the citizens on the development of vaccines, vaccination progress, and were addressing queries related to Covid-19 vaccination.

Media briefings by top echelons of health administrations in India were made into a daily feature. Social media channels of the Union Ministry of Health and Family Welfare became the go-to source for the public to receive authentic information on the Covid-19 vaccination program.

The official Twitter (now X) handle of the Ministry of Health (@MoHFW_INDIA) witnessed significantly high addition of new followers every month since January 2020 with an average 50,000 followers being added every month (Fig. 5.1 shows Monthly New Followers added on official Twitter handle between January 2020 till June 2023).

Proactive content creation was really engaging awaited by public at large. Health experts were invited to be a part of #VaccineVarta and #CovidCharcha, weekly chat shows on MoHFW's Twitter handle, wherein real-time responses were given by experts on queries raised by public. Bytes and messages from these experts were further cross promoted on other platforms like Facebook, Share chat, Public, and community radio stations.

Multiple other digital campaigns were planned on a regular interval with a focus on vaccination drive like How to book a Covid-19 vaccination appointment and vaccine Hesitancy.

Similarly, the Ministry's official YouTube saw very high reach on educational videos on Covid-19 vaccination and registration on the Co-WIN digital platform. Some of these videos have over 20 million views. These all have been organic without spending any money to increase reach and followers on any of the social media

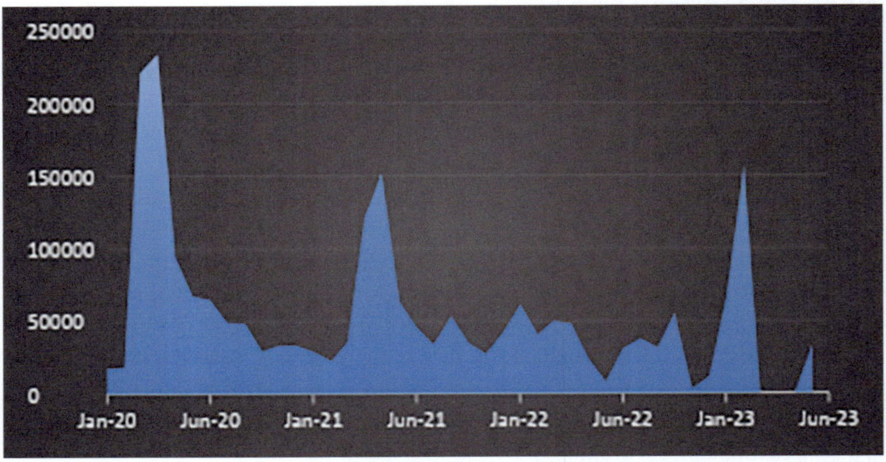

Fig. 5.1 Monthly New Followers added on official Twitter handle between January 2020 and June 2023. (Source: https://x.com/MoHFW_INDIA)

platforms. (Covid-19 awareness videos and their views can be accessed on YouTube through the link "https://www.youtube.com/@mohfwindia/videos").

Electronic media supported the entire program. They invited technical experts to address public queries and other issues around the vaccination discourse through panel discussions, debates, etc. Apart from private channels public broadcasters like DD news, LSTV (now Sansad TV), All India Radio were all engaged.

Mewat, a district in state of Haryana has been a vaccine-hesitant district from the beginning for routine immunization as well. Similar hesitancy was reported in the district during early phases of Covid-19 vaccination program. Here, one of the innovations used was involvement of community radio, Alfaz-e-Mewat FM 107.8.

Learnings from Polio campaign, Intensified Mission Indradhanush campaign (IMI), and MR vaccination campaigns were inbuilt in the Covid-19 vaccination communication strategy. Positive participation of the local religious and community leaders and mass appeal by them during campaign was part of the communication strategy. Thereby such mass leaders became critical stakeholder in spreading the right messages around vaccination and addressing hesitancy. This strategy was very useful in vaccine-hesitant districts like Mewat, and north-eastern states like Meghalaya, Mizoram, Arunachal Pradesh, and Tripura.

Communication for Covid-19 pandemic and the subsequent largest vaccination program is a case study in public health communication. Political leadership in the entire country led from the front, engaged public on a regular basis to make the program a true Jan Andolan.

Equipped with a well-thought out and scientific communication strategy, along with exemplary work of health workers, frontline workers, scientists, along with active participation of citizens in all states and union territories ensured that world's largest population cohort received over 2.2 million doses of lifesaving Covid-19 vaccines.

The world's largest Covid-19 vaccination effort has been very well articulated up by Cynthia McCaffrey, UNICEF India Representative, "The State of the World's Children 2023 report highlights India as one of the countries with the highest vaccine confidence in the world. This is a recognition of the Government of India's political and social commitment and demonstrates that the #largestvaccinesdrive during the pandemic has paid off in building confidence and strengthening systems for routine immunization to vaccinate every child."[10]

Indeed, a once-in-a-century public health crisis like pandemic of Covid-19 was successfully defeated through people's movement and active participation.

[10] https://www.unicef.org/india/press-releases/unicef-flagship-report-highlights-new-data-indias-gains-vaccines-confidence-amidst#:~:text=%E2%80%9CThe%20State%20of%20the%20World's,vaccine%20confidence%20in%20the%20world.

5.1 Conclusion

In the realm of public health, effective health communication plays a pivotal role by bridging the information gap among citizens. It serves as a catalyst for raising awareness, fostering behavior change, and minimizing risks. This dynamic tool empowers individuals to make informed decisions about their health, creating a foundation for healthier lifestyles. Particularly during emergencies like the Covid-19 pandemic, precise communication is vital for risk perception management, offering guidance, and preventing undue panic. Health communication, reinforced by social norms and peer influence, stands as a safeguard against misinformation, ensuring accurate information dissemination.

The success of India's Covid-19 vaccination program exemplifies the power of communication. World's largest mass vaccination campaign demonstrated a two-way communication approach involving the community, from the grassroots to policymakers. Through leveraging digital platforms, news outlets, and social media, India engaged its smartphone-savvy population. "Jan Aandolan" emphasized key practices like mask wearing and hand hygiene, underscoring the importance of engagement.

Clear communication efforts were instrumental in overcoming vaccine hesitancy and misinformation challenges. Collaborations with credible sources and endorsement from experts fortified the vaccination drive's credibility. The strategy's multi-dimensional approach covered crucial areas: providing vaccine information, addressing eagerness and hesitancy, and promoting Covid-19 appropriate Behavior. A structured governance mechanism ensured timely and transparent information dissemination down to the district level, enhancing vaccine confidence.

In response to the "infodemic," characterized by rapid misinformation spread, India employed a National Media Rapid Response cell, fact-check units, and expert-led fact check videos. By swiftly addressing falsehoods and harnessing traditional and digital media, India contained misinformation's impact on its vaccination campaign.

Key influencers were engaged through platforms like #VaccineVarta and #CovidCharcha, enhancing information outreach. Community radio, like in past during the successful Polio campaign, effectively addressed vaccine hesitancy in areas like Mewat. The involvement of religious and community leaders bolstered the strategy's impact, particularly in hesitant regions.

The culmination of these efforts led to the world's highest vaccine confidence rates, as recognized by international bodies. Through the active participation of citizens and strategic communication, India navigated a once-in-a-century public health crisis, proving the resilience and potency of collaborative health communication in building healthier societies.

Media Engagement: A Pillar of Success in India's Covid-19 Vaccination Drive

6

Manisha Verma and Ankur Lahoty

Abstract

The global Covid-19 pandemic has been a watershed moment where countries have learned and implemented several innovative interventions not only in public health but also in crisis communication. In India, the Union Ministry of Health & Family Welfare center-staged risk communication with a sharp focus on social and behavioral change communication. Strategic communication plans were drawn as an integral part of health crisis management, involving multiple stakeholders and media platforms to optimize their potential. This chapter will examine these strategies at a close quarter and analyze how they proved to be effective tools of health emergency management. Learnings that emerge can prove to be valuable underpinnings for an efficacious risk communication plan for such health emergencies.

Keywords

Covid-19 · Vaccination · Pandemic · Public health · Infodemic · Behavior change communication · Risk communication · India · Health Ministry

The outbreak of Covid-19 in late 2019 marked a defining moment in modern history, as the world grappled with an unprecedented public health crisis. The Covid-19 pandemic, caused by the novel coronavirus SARS-CoV-2, quickly spread across continents, overwhelming healthcare systems and disrupting economies. As countries faced the relentless challenges posed by the virus, India emerged as a major

M. Verma (✉)
Union Ministry of Health and Family Welfare, New Delhi, India

A. Lahoty
Union Ministry of Information and Broadcasting, Guwahati, Assam, India

M. Agnani et al. (eds.), *India's Covid-19 Vaccine Drive*,
https://doi.org/10.1007/978-981-95-8138-2_6

battleground in the fight against the pandemic. In this crucible of uncertainty, the Ministry of Health and Family Welfare took center stage, leading the charge to combat Covid-19 and chart a path toward recovery.

This chapter delves into the media strategy adopted by the Ministry of Health and Family Welfare and Press Information Bureau (PIB) for the world's largest Covid-19 Vaccination Program in highlighting the strategic measures, decisive actions, and innovative approaches that positioned India as a global case study in Covid-19 vaccination.

The Covid-19 pandemic presented an unprecedented challenge to the global community, requiring swift and effective communication strategies to control the spread of the virus and encourage vaccination. In the context of India's diverse and vast population, the role of media has been indispensable. The media played a vital role in disseminating accurate information, raising awareness, and addressing various challenges faced during the Covid-19 vaccination drive. Given India's linguistic, cultural, and regional diversity, the media's ability to communicate in multiple languages and reach diverse communities has been crucial.

Social media platforms like Twitter, Facebook, YouTube, and Instagram emerged as powerful tools for information dissemination, community engagement, and behavior change communication. Through engaging and informative content, these platforms have helped raise awareness about Covid-19 vaccination campaigns, transcending linguistic and cultural barriers. The use of social media allowed the media to interact directly with the public, answer queries, and address concerns promptly. This two-way communication not only disseminated accurate information but also helped address vaccine hesitancy, and combat misinformation.

Recognizing the pivotal role of communication, the Ministry of Health and Family Welfare in collaboration with the Press Information Bureau (PIB) under Ministry of Information & Broadcasting adopted a robust and multi-faceted 360° multi-stakeholder media strategy. This strategy was designed to address various challenges such as vaccine hesitancy, misinformation, Fake News, and bolster public engagement.

Daily press releases on Covid-19 situation, vaccination progress, and press rebuttals on fake news ensured timely dissemination of accurate information. They allowed key stakeholders, health experts, and senior officials to interact with journalists, providing transparent updates and addressing queries. Informal meetings with media and key stakeholders fostered a deeper understanding of government efforts and decisions. Extensive use of social media platforms, including Twitter spaces, Facebook live, and YouTube videos, enabled real-time interaction with the public, sharing critical information and combating misinformation.

Regional media and community radio were actively engaged to reach diverse populations. Additionally, organizing regular press tours to Covid-19 vaccine-related facilities showcased the robust vaccination infrastructure and inspired public confidence. This comprehensive media strategy played a pivotal role in India's successful Covid-19 vaccination drive, and addressing various challenges that arose during the same. The use of vernacular languages has been instrumental in reaching diverse linguistic communities, making information inclusive and relatable.

The Ministry leveraged an array of media platforms (print, electronic, and social media) to reach various strata of society. Television channels served as a significant conduit for public service announcements, while radio broadcasts targeted remote regions. Print media played a role in educating the population, while social media platforms facilitated direct interaction and real-time updates. Role of Public Broadcasters, Doordarshan News, and AIR News was of paramount importance. Doordarshan and All India Radio along with the media units of Information & Broadcasting Ministry such as Press Information Bureau, Central Bureau of Communication (CBC), Publications Division played a crucial role in reaching the last mile through their vast network. The various media tools deployed during the vaccination drive were as follows.

6.1 Press Releases and Press Rebuttals

Daily press releases served as a crucial source of official information on the Covid-19 situation, vaccination progress, and government guidelines. These releases were instrumental in keeping the media and the public well informed. Additionally, press rebuttals were promptly issued to counter misinformation and fake news, ensuring the accuracy of information circulating in the media.

More than 10,000 Press releases and 400 press rebuttals were issued during the period. All Press releases were translated by the regional offices of the Press Information Bureau in regional languages and circulated through WhatsApp groups across the country in real time.

6.2 Press Conferences

Regular press conferences were held, led by key stakeholders, health experts, and senior officials from the Ministry of Health and Family Welfare. These conferences provided an opportunity to address queries from journalists and clarify any doubts on Covid-19-related matters. Transparent and timely communication fostered trust between the government and the media. More than 1000 Press conferences were organized by PIB during the period, and all were telecast live on social media platforms too.

6.3 Informal Meetings with Key Stakeholders

Informal meetings between the media and key stakeholders, such as the Health Minister, Member Health NITI Aayog, Secretary Health & Family Welfare, DG Indian Council of Medical Research, and other senior health officials, allowed for more in-depth discussions on various Covid-19 vaccination-related topics. This facilitated a better understanding of the government's efforts and decisions, leading to more comprehensive media coverage. Webinars, Video Conferences, conferences, etc., with media and key stakeholders were organized.

6.4 Interaction with Regional Media, Including Community Radio

The media strategy emphasized engaging regional media, recognizing its role in reaching remote and underserved communities. Regular interactions with regional journalists and community radio stations ensured that accurate information and guidelines were disseminated to every corner of the country. More than 50 regional media interactions were organized in collaboration with the Ministry of Information & Broadcasting, Doordarshan, All India Radio, Press Information Bureau, Central Bureau of Communication, UNICEF, WHO, BMGF, etc.

6.5 Facilitating Interviews, Articles, Short Bytes of Doctors/Policymakers/Health Experts

During the Covid-19 pandemic and vaccination drive, the Ministry of Health and Family Welfare played a pivotal role in facilitating media engagement with prominent figures such as doctors, policymakers, and health experts. A list of experts was prepared with contact details and media outlets were granted access to health experts and policymakers, allowing them to seek clarifications, gather insights, and share credible information with the public in addition to writing articles and Opinion editorials on various issues of Covid-19 management and vaccination.

6.6 Extensive Use of Social Media

Understanding the power of social media in reaching a vast audience, the Ministry extensively used platforms like Twitter (now X platform), Facebook, Instagram, Public, Koo, and YouTube. Twitter Spaces were utilized for real-time interactions, enabling experts and officials to address public concerns directly. Facebook/Instagram live sessions and YouTube videos were employed to create informative and engaging content, making vital information accessible to the masses.

6.7 Organizing Regular Press Tours to Covid-19 Vaccine Facilities

To build confidence in vaccination, the Ministry organized regular press tours to Covid-19 vaccine-related facilities. Journalists were given first-hand access to vaccine manufacturing units, distribution centers, and vaccination sites. These tours provided valuable insight into the robust infrastructure and processes involved in the vaccination drive. In a one of its kind interventions for media outreach, the concept of Knowledge Sharing Workshops/Press tours of national media health Journalists to various facilities of the Health Ministry were organized. Visits of the National media delegation to CDL Kasauli, NIV Pune, NIN Hyderabad, Bharat Biotech Plant, etc., in collaboration with ICMR were organized.

6.8 Communication Campaigns for Covid-19 Vaccination

Throughout the vaccination drive, the Ministry undertook numerous communication activities. Engaging infographics and visually appealing content were created to disseminate critical information effectively. Personalized video messages from healthcare experts fostered trust and credibility. Several communication campaigns were devised in collaboration with States NHM officials, AIIMS, ICMR, and other key stakeholders for promoting use of Covid-19 Vaccination. Campaigns such as "Har Ghar Dastak" for Vaccination and 100 Crore milestone campaign were devised and implemented successfully. These campaigns created a positive perception of the Government.

6.9 Collaborations and Partnerships

Collaboration was central to the media strategy's success. Engaging media organizations, NGOs, community leaders, and influencers broadened the reach of Covid-19 vaccination–related messages. Public-private partnerships allowed for resource optimization and innovative approaches to communication. Some of the highlights of various collaborations are as follows:

The Ministry forged zero budget collaborations with over 40 private companies such as Zomato, Swiggy, Mother Dairy, Vistara, and Paytm for amplifying the key messages on Covid-19-appropriate behavior and vaccination.

As a part of digital media and industry-ministry collaboration initiatives, for the first time the Ministry collaborated with social media organizations and introduced innovative and emerging modes of communication such as Twitter Spaces, FB/Instagram Live, Google doodle, My gov quiz, YouTube sessions of Health Minister, and key officials. In addition, digital marketing was undertaken through complementary ad grants received from Twitter, Google, FB, etc.

Further, celebrity influencer engagement on social media was undertaken on a war footing. Influencers such as Technical Guruji were engaged for Covid-19 communication messages.

The Ministry worked in close coordination with UNICEF, UNDP, State Governments, NGOs, Civil society, WHO, BMGF, and MyGov, which amplified the Govt's efforts.

Media engagement has played the role of a strong pillar in the notable success of India's Covid-19 Vaccination Drive is evident from following two case study examples.

The first case study is related to countering international campaigns against Indian-origin vaccines, especially Covaxin is relevant to quote here. As India proudly launched its indigenous Covid-19 vaccine, Covaxin along with Covishield, it faced an unforeseen challenge—a relentless campaign spreading misinformation and casting doubt on the safety and efficacy of Indian vaccines. False claims disparaging the origin, manufacturing process, and regulatory approval process of Covaxin threatened to undermine public trust in the domestically developed vaccine.

The Ministry of Health and Family Welfare swiftly devised a comprehensive strategy to counter the international misinformation campaign and debunk fake news surrounding Indian-origin vaccines. Realizing the importance of credible communication and engaging with global media, the Ministry adopted a proactive approach to address concerns and present accurate information. The Ministry through the Ministry of External Affairs leveraged diplomatic channels to provide transparent information about Covaxin's development, manufacturing, and regulatory processes. They shared data from clinical trials, peer-reviewed publications, and approvals from regulatory authorities, emphasizing the rigorous scientific evaluation that Covaxin had undergone. The Ministry also collaborated with Indian embassies and missions worldwide to address media queries and concerns raised by foreign governments.

The Ministry's steadfast efforts in addressing international concerns yielded positive outcomes. As accurate information prevailed, the doubts surrounding Covaxin began to dissipate, and the vaccine's credibility was reaffirmed globally. Several international media organizations and health authorities retracted misleading reports and recognized the robustness of Indian vaccine development.

By countering the international campaign against Indian-origin vaccines, especially Covaxin, the Ministry effectively safeguarded the reputation of Indian vaccine research and development. This case study underscores the importance of evidence-based communication, global engagement, and strategic diplomacy in dispelling misinformation and protecting the reputation of critical public health interventions.

The second case study is about the Vaccine Maitri Initiative—India's Commitment to Global Vaccine Equity. As the Covid-19 pandemic swept across the world, access to vaccines became a critical global challenge. India, as the world's largest vaccine manufacturers, faced the dilemma of meeting its domestic vaccination needs while also extending support to other nations struggling with limited vaccine supplies. The challenge lay in ensuring equitable vaccine distribution globally while safeguarding the health of its own citizens.

In response to the global crisis, India launched the "Vaccine Maitri" initiative, reflecting its commitment to vaccine equity and solidarity with other nations. The initiative aimed to supply vaccines to low- and middle-income countries, especially those in the South Asian region and beyond, to help combat the pandemic collectively.

The Vaccine Maitri initiative garnered significant media attention, both within India and internationally. While the global community hailed India's commitment to vaccine equity, the media closely scrutinized the availability of vaccines domestically and questioned whether the initiative would hinder India's own vaccination drive.

In response to media queries, the Ministry of External Affairs and Ministry of Health and Family Welfare reiterated India's pledge to ensure adequate vaccine supplies for its citizens. They communicated that India's vaccine diplomacy was based on the principle of "Vasudhaiva Kutumbakam" (the world is one family), and the country was confident in meeting both domestic and international vaccine demands. India's efforts to balance domestic vaccination needs with global responsibilities required careful media management. The government emphasized that as vaccine production capacities increased, India could cater to both aspects without compromising its domestic vaccination targets.

Despite facing initial challenges due to limited vaccine supply, the Vaccine Maitri initiative eventually bore fruit. India successfully supplied millions of doses of Covid-19 vaccines to over 95 countries worldwide, including neighboring countries, African nations, and countries in Latin America and the Caribbean.

The media's portrayal of India's vaccine diplomacy evolved over time. As the initiative's impact became evident, the media recognized India's pivotal role in supporting global vaccine equity. Media reports highlighted the gratitude expressed by recipient countries and lauded India's contributions in a global effort to ensure equitable access to vaccines. The Vaccine Maitri initiative not only bolstered India's standing on the global stage but also showcased the nation's humanitarian values and commitment to international cooperation during times of crisis. It reaffirmed India's position as the "Pharmacy of the World," providing affordable and accessible vaccines to those in need.

In conclusion, the Vaccine Maitri initiative exemplifies India's resolve to promote vaccine equity and uphold global solidarity despite facing domestic challenges. This initiative underscores the importance of effective media management in navigating sensitive issues and communicating the balance between meeting domestic vaccination needs and supporting global efforts. India's Vaccine Maitri initiative remains an inspiration for countries worldwide, demonstrating that even with limited resources, collective action and a spirit of compassion can pave the way for a healthier and more equitable world.

6.10 Challenges Faced During Covid-19 Vaccination Drive

During the Covid-19 vaccination process, the country faced several challenges that required careful communication and media engagement. Some of these challenges included the following:

I. Vaccine Hesitancy As India embarked on its mission to vaccinate its vast population against Covid-19, it confronted a multitude of vaccination challenges that permeated society. Vaccine hesitancy was a significant challenge during the initial phase of vaccination drive. Misinformation and rumors created myths and misconceptions which ranged from irrational fears to illogical claims and even superstitious beliefs, creating significant barriers to achieving widespread immunization in certain segments of the population. Overcoming vaccine hesitancy required targeted communication campaigns, education about vaccine safety and efficacy, and the involvement of trusted community leaders and influencers.

To combat vaccine hesitancy and address the myths surrounding Covid-19 vaccines, the Ministry of Health and Family Welfare launched a targeted "Facts Vs Myth" campaign and "Har Ghar Dastak" campaign.

The "Facts Vs Myth" campaign aimed to provide evidence-based information and dispel misconceptions through clear and concise communication. Some of the Myths and Facts given are as follows.

Figure 6.1 shows some of these press releases under the "Facts Vs Myth" campaign.

Myth: Vaccines contain microchips for tracking individuals.
Fact: Vaccines do not contain any microchips. This baseless claim spread fear of government surveillance, causing vaccine hesitancy.
Myth: Vaccines alter DNA and genetic makeup.
Fact: Vaccines work by triggering an immune response to protect against the virus. They do not alter an individual's DNA.

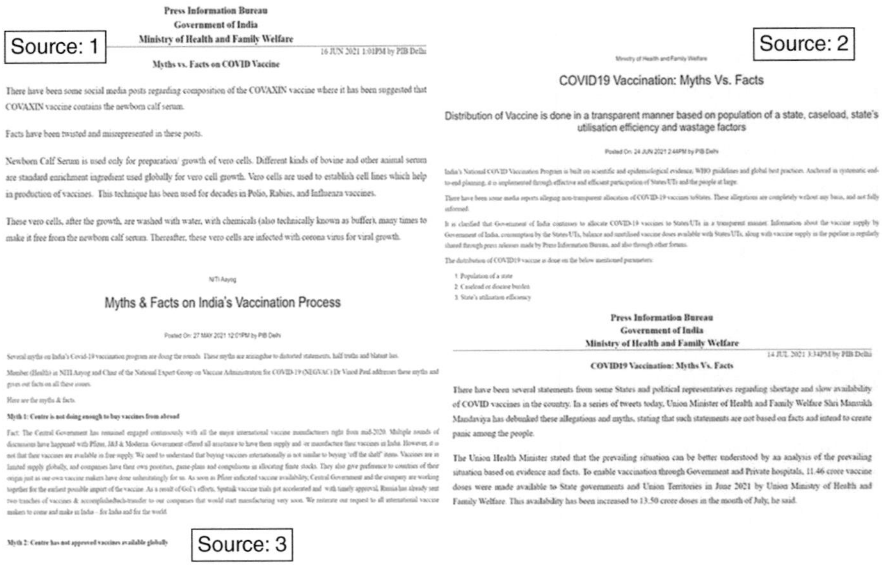

Source: 1

Press Information Bureau
Government of India
Ministry of Health and Family Welfare

16 JUN 2021 1:01PM by PIB Delhi

Myths vs. Facts on COVID Vaccine

There have been some social media posts regarding composition of the COVAXIN vaccine where it has been suggested that COVAXIN vaccine contains the newborn calf serum.

Facts have been twisted and misrepresented in these posts.

Newborn Calf Serum is used only for preparation/ growth of vero cells. Different kinds of bovine and other animal serum are standard enrichment ingredient used globally for vero cell growth. Vero cells are used to establish cell lines which help in production of vaccines. This technique has been used for decades in Polio, Rabies, and Influenza vaccines.

These vero cells, after the growth, are washed with water, with chemicals (also technically known as buffer), many times to make it free from the newborn calf serum. Thereafter, these vero cells are infected with corona virus for viral growth.

NITI Aayog

Myths & Facts on India's Vaccination Process

Posted On: 27 MAY 2021 12:01PM by PIB Delhi

Myth 1: Centre is not doing enough to buy vaccines from abroad

Myth 2: Centre has not approved vaccines available globally

Source: 3

Source: 2

Ministry of Health and Family Welfare

COVID19 Vaccination: Myths Vs. Facts

Distribution of Vaccine is done in a transparent manner based on population of a state, caseload, state's utilisation efficiency and wastage factors

Posted On: 24 JUN 2021 2:44PM by PIB Delhi

The distribution of COVID19 vaccine is done on the below mentioned parameters:

1. Population of a state
2. Caseload or disease burden
3. State's utilisation efficiency

Press Information Bureau
Government of India
Ministry of Health and Family Welfare

14 JUL 2021 3:34PM by PIB Delhi

COVID19 Vaccination: Myths Vs. Facts

There have been several statements from some States and political representatives regarding shortage and slow availability of COVID vaccines in the country. In a series of tweets today, Union Minister of Health and Family Welfare Shri Mansukh Mandaviya has debunked these allegations and myths, stating that such statements are not based on facts and intend to create panic among the people.

The Union Health Minister stated that the prevailing situation can be better understood by an analysis of the prevailing situation based on evidence and facts. To enable vaccination through Government and Private hospitals, 11.46 crore vaccine doses were made available to State governments and Union Territories in June 2021 by Union Ministry of Health and Family Welfare. This availability has been increased to 13.50 crore doses in the month of July, he said.

Fig. 6.1 Press releases of MoHFW under the "Facts Vs Myth" campaign. Source 1: https://pib.gov.in/PressReleasePage.aspx?PRID=1727462. Source 2: https://pib.gov.in/PressReleasePage.aspx?PRID=1730003. Source 3: https://pib.gov.in/PressReleasePage.aspx?PRID=1722078

Myth: Natural immunity is superior to vaccination.
Fact: While natural immunity from a previous infection may offer protection, vaccination enhances immunity and provides more reliable defense against severe illness and new variants.
Myth: Vaccines can lead to infertility.
Fact: Extensive research shows no evidence of vaccines causing infertility. They are safe for individuals trying to conceive or during pregnancy.
Myth: Vaccines can transmit the virus to others.
Fact: Vaccines cannot cause Covid-19 as they do not contain the live virus. They stimulate the immune system to recognize and fight the virus if exposed.
Myth: Only elderly people need vaccination.
Fact: Covid-19 can affect people of all age groups. Vaccination is essential for everyone to build immunity and protect against severe illness and transmission.
Myth: People who have recovered from Covid-19 don't need vaccination.
Fact: Vaccination is still recommended for individuals who have recovered from Covid-19. It boosts immunity and provides protection against reinfection.
Myth: People with underlying health conditions should avoid vaccination.
Fact: On the contrary, individuals with underlying health conditions, such as diabetes or hypertension, are encouraged to get vaccinated as they are at higher risk for severe Covid-19.
Myth: Vaccines are not effective against new variants.
Fact: Vaccines remain effective against most variants of the virus, providing protection against severe illness and reducing transmission.

Collaborating with health experts, public figures, and credible media partners, the Ministry launched an information campaign across various media platforms. Through television, radio, social media, and print, they presented factual data and testimonials from vaccinated individuals. Community leaders and influencers also played a vital role in endorsing vaccination and debunking myths.

The "Har Ghar Dastak" campaign aimed to ensure that all adults in India receive their first dose of the Covid-19 vaccine, while also tracking and motivating those due for their second dose to complete their vaccination schedule. Translating to "knocking at every door," the campaign involved healthcare workers conducting door-to-door vaccinations, with particular emphasis on districts where less than 50% of the eligible population had been inoculated.

Through this campaign, the frontline health workers addressed various issues preventing people from getting vaccinated. The initiative also involved collaborating with local religious and community leaders, as well as other agencies and organizations, such as the Central Statistics Office (CSO), non-government organizations (NGOs), and the National Service Scheme (NSS), to encourage vaccine uptake. Multimedia information, education, and communication (IEC) campaigns were designed to combat anti-vaccine rumors and replicate successful vaccination strategies from high-coverage districts.

The "Facts Vs Myth" campaign and "Har Ghar Dastak campaign" achieved significant success in debunking vaccination myths and increasing public confidence in Covid-19 vaccines. Vaccination rates increased in regions where the campaign was particularly focused, leading to higher vaccine acceptance and improved vaccine coverage. In fact, India's successful vaccination campaign is a global case study. The single day vaccination coverage of India was more than the total vaccination of many developed countries. In fact, when the western world was witnessing protest vaccination, India was witnessing community support for vaccination from all walks of life.

II. Adverse Events Following Immunization (AEFI) Vaccination campaigns encountered instances of adverse events following immunization. While these events were relatively rare and often unrelated to the vaccines, they generated concerns among the public. Communicating transparently about the investigations, safety protocols, and the overall benefit-risk balance of vaccines was essential to address vaccine safety fears.

III. Addressing Misinformation and Fake News The infodemic of misinformation and fake news was rampant during the vaccination process. Countering misinformation through fact-based communication, collaborating with reputable media partners, and engaging social media platforms to curb the spread of fake news were essential in managing this challenge. PIB Fact Check on X platform (Twitter previously) proved to be a game changer in addressing Fake News. In addition to this, a special series of Myths vs Facts was initiated by the Ministry to counter fake narratives as explained above.

IV. Language and Cultural Diversity India's diverse linguistic and cultural landscape added complexity to communication efforts. Tailoring messages to resonate with different linguistic and cultural groups was necessary to ensure broad understanding and compliance with public health guidelines.

V. Digital Divide and Information Access The digital divide in India posed challenges in accessing accurate information for certain communities. Ensuring information was available through multiple channels, including community radio, print media, and traditional modes, was necessary to bridge this gap.

Overcoming these challenges required a well-coordinated and adaptive media strategy. The Ministry of Health and Family Welfare, in collaboration with media partners, adopted innovative approaches to address each of these issues, leading to India's success in managing Covid-19 and promoting vaccination.

6.11 Monitoring and Evaluation

As highlighted above, ensuring swift and accurate communication was crucial to combat misinformation and manage public perception effectively. Daily feedback on important issues and analysis of media reports (editorials, perspectives) were to be the main components of monitoring and evaluation. Data analysis, surveys, and feedback mechanisms were conceptualized to get valuable insights. Further, to ensure the media strategy's effectiveness, the Ministry needed to closely monitor its impact. Ministry of Health and Family Welfare also recognized the need to respond rapidly to media queries, address rumors, and provide timely updates.

As a solution to this problem, Ministry conceptualized the National Media Rapid Response Cell (NMRRC) War Room, a specialized team comprising communication experts, health professionals, and media liaisons. The NMRRC was equipped with real-time data and the latest information to respond to media queries across the country on all the available media platforms. The team was trained to craft clear and consistent messaging and work closely with media outlets to disseminate accurate updates.

The NMRRC established a centralized communication hub that streamlined information flow between the Ministry and the media. Journalists could reach out to the NMRRC 24/7 for expert interviews, official statements, and fact-checking. The Cell collaborated with media outlets to promote Covid-19 vaccination, facilitate interviews with healthcare experts, and dispel misinformation.

The NMRRC's efficient functioning significantly improved media engagement, ensuring timely and accurate information dissemination. By providing a direct line of communication with the Ministry, journalists had access to reliable sources, reducing the spread of misinformation. The NMRRC played a crucial role in increasing awareness, building public trust and positive sentiment, and thereby contributing to increased vaccination rates.

6.12 Learnings and Future Recommendations

The media strategy's success lay in its adaptability and comprehensiveness. The media engagement by the Ministry of Health and Family Welfare in India's Covid-19 management and vaccination drive has provided valuable insights for future crisis communication. Timely and transparent communication, tailored messages for diverse audiences, and leveraging social media have proven crucial. Collaborating with credible media partners, addressing vaccine hesitancy effectively, and balancing sensitivity with authoritative messaging have been essential. Continuous monitoring and evaluation of communication efforts, as well as strengthening digital infrastructure, are key takeaways for successful crisis communication in the face of unprecedented challenges. Additionally, building strong relationships with journalists and media organizations can bolster crisis communication efforts.

6.13 Conclusion

In response to the unprecedented challenges posed by the Covid-19 pandemic, India's response under Ministry of Health and Family Welfare, in collaboration with the Press Information Bureau (PIB), emerged as a beacon of hope and success. A pivotal pillar in this extraordinary journey was execution of a comprehensive media strategy to effectively communicate and manage the world's largest Covid-19 Vaccination Program. This strategy encompassed a range of media platforms, including traditional media and social media, to address challenges like vaccine hesitancy, misinformation, and public engagement.

By effectively leveraging a combination of media tools, the Ministry of Health and Family Welfare successfully addressed challenges, built public trust, countered misinformation, and ensured the successful implementation of India's Covid-19 vaccination drive. This multifaceted media strategy serves as a global case study for communication strategies during a health crisis, highlighting the importance of tailored approaches for diverse populations and the power of collaboration between government agencies and media entities.

Two case studies highlight the strategy's impact: Countering International Campaigns against Indian-Origin Vaccines & Vaccine Maitri Initiative for ensuring Global Vaccine Equity. The key learnings of this entire effort are as follows:

- Adaptability and comprehensiveness are key.
- Timely, transparent, and tailored communication is crucial.
- Collaborating with credible media partners is effective.
- Balancing sensitivity with authoritative messaging is essential.
- Continuous monitoring and evaluation of communication efforts is vital.
- Strengthening digital infrastructure is important for crisis communication success.

In summary, India's successful media strategy hinged on collaboration, innovative communication, and strategic diplomacy. The initiatives showcased the importance of evidence-based communication in dispelling misinformation and the power of global solidarity in addressing public health challenges. The lessons learned from this experience will undoubtedly shape future communication, and media engagement strategies.

Journey Through Legal Lens: Legal Battles to Administer Over 220 Crore Vaccine Doses in Record Time

7

Ashish B. Chakraborty and Nilesh Kumar Jain

Abstract

This chapter sketches India's legal and governance challenges during the Covid-19 pandemic, emphasizing the significant role played by Indian Judiciary in supporting the National Covid-19 vaccination Program. It portrays the Indian Judiciary as a guardian of constitutional principles, balancing public health needs with individual liberties under Article 21 of the Constitution of India. Key areas of judicial intervention included policy reviews, vaccine mandates, emergency approvals, and equitable distribution strategies. Judiciary reviewed critical policies like vaccine pricing and phased administration of vaccines, digital divides and advocated for vulnerable groups like homeless, elderly, bedridden individuals, migrants, and people without ID card. The judiciary also scrutinized regulatory frameworks, emphasizing transparency in vaccine approvals and adverse event following immunization reporting mechanism. Challenges like certificate corrections, booster dose timing, and international travel requirements were also resolved through legal directives. Highlighting collaborative governance, this chapter celebrates India's achievement of delivering over 220 crore vaccine doses within 2 years, showcasing an extraordinary union of judicial oversight, government resolve, and public participation.

Keywords

Judiciary · Legal directive · Constitution of India · Judicial intervention · Policy review · Regulatory framework · Judicial oversight · Vaccine mandate

A. B. Chakraborty (✉) · N. K. Jain
Ministry of Health and Family Welfare, New Delhi, India
e-mail: ashish.bchakraborty@gov.in

M. Agnani et al. (eds.), *India's Covid-19 Vaccine Drive*,
https://doi.org/10.1007/978-981-95-8138-2_7

The bedrock of a thriving democracy lies upon its four pillars: Legislative, Executive, Judiciary, and Media. Judiciary in India stands resolute and independent, representing a bastion of justice where individuals and institutions seek solace for their grievances. With a rich history of active involvement in pivotal national events, the Indian Judiciary has emerged not as a mere observer but as a proactive force championing the cause of common citizens.

When the Covid-19 pandemic swept across the nation, the Indian Judiciary exhibited a remarkable zeal, stepping forward to comprehend the crisis and ensure the government's actions were just and beneficial to every citizen. In the intricate dance of India's National Covid-19 Vaccination Program, the Judiciary assumed a pivotal role. While the executive branch bore the primary responsibility for implementation, the Judiciary emerged as a vigilant sentinel, ensuring the program's execution adhered to the principles of fairness, equity, and transparency.

Beyond a support pillar, the Judiciary showcased an exemplary proactive stance. The Honorable courts exercised their jurisdiction with sagacity, scrutinizing policy measures for reasonableness, safeguarding against arbitrary actions, and upholding the sacrosanct right to life for all. A distinctive dialogic jurisdiction emerged, offering a platform for diverse stakeholders to raise constitutional concerns regarding Covid-19 vaccination. This open-court dialogue facilitated rigorous evaluation of policies, ensuring they not only stood up to constitutional scrutiny but also upheld the tenets of protecting life and liberty.

The Judiciary emerged as the guardian of constitutional principles, diligently safeguarding fundamental rights, conducting meticulous judicial reviews of governmental actions, and deftly balancing the scales between public health imperatives and individual freedoms.

This commitment resonated across the diverse landscape of India's judicial structure. Each state boasts its own esteemed High Court as the apex legal authority, providing a refuge for citizens common threads of grievances, such as vaccine availability, safety concerns, emergency approvals, and the rights of persons with disabilities, wove a tapestry of legal action across multiple High Courts, echoing the resonance of shared concerns in every corner of the nation.

In essence, the Indian Judiciary, ensconced in its role as a sturdy pillar of democracy, to safeguard fundamental rights, scrutinize policies, and strike a harmonious chord between public welfare and individual liberties.

When the pandemic engulfed the nation, the officers of Immunization Division of Department of Health & Family Welfare, Government of India, worked tirelessly to ensure that the Covid-19 vaccine reached every state, ensuring equity in the face of adversity. Coincidentally, it was during this tumultuous period that the populace's anxiety unleashed a torrent of court cases. Traditionally, the Immunization division encountered a mere handful of cases each year—one to three, to be precise. Ordinarily, there was ample time to prepare before the next hearing. However, the pandemic era obliterated such luxuries, thrusting the technical officers into a maelstrom of responsibilities.

During the pandemic, the Immunization Division found itself besieged by over 125 court cases within the span of a single year. Such a tempest of legal challenges was unparalleled in the division's history. Remarkably, this surge coincided with the Judiciary's extraordinary transformation. Court hearings took place on a priority basis, even on a day-to-day cadence. The Judiciary's system of releasing the next day's case list in the evening catalyzed a whirlwind of preparation, often extending into the early hours of the morning. Thanks to technological marvels like Google Meet and Zoom, meetings could transcend traditional working hours, enabling the finalization of counter affidavits in unconventional times.

Guiding the ship of the Ministry of Health and Family Welfare was the Secretary of Health, the helm of leadership. Each draft of a court case destined for the esteemed Supreme Court underwent meticulous scrutiny by the Secretary of Health. Similarly, cases set for the Hon'ble High Courts received the careful review of Additional Secretary overseeing Covid-19 vaccination. Navigating the legal landscape was the Health Ministry's legal cell, commanded by a Joint Secretary (Legal), ably supported by three legal consultants: one each for Reproductive and Child Health, National Health Mission, and Non-Communicable Disease divisions in the Ministry of Health and Family Welfare.

Days often dawned with multiple cases awaiting their moment in different high courts. Remarkably, there was an instance when a staggering ten cases were slated for the very next day. This scenario necessitated multiple responses, all to be meticulously vetted by various echelons of the hierarchy within a single day. The sheer volume of cases strained the system, prompting a strategic decision to fortify the Immunization Division. This marked a pivotal moment: the Immunization Division, for the first time in the annals of the Health Ministry, had its own legal cell. This power-packed ensemble consisted of a Deputy Commissioner-level technical officer, a technical consultant, and a legal consultant, all singularly dedicated to navigating the labyrinth of court cases.

In the face of this whirlwind, every level of the hierarchy rallied with a sense of purpose. Evening discussions extending beyond 9 pm, Sunday deliberations led by the Secretary of Health for cases heading to the Supreme Court—these became emblematic of the Ministry's unparalleled dedication. Amidst the turbulence, a remarkable feat emerged: despite the unanticipated barrage of cases, the tight schedules, the cross-jurisdictional intricacies, and the unusual working hours, the Health Ministry emerged unscathed. Not a single contempt of court case marred the ministry's record, a testament to their extraordinary achievement. The saga of the Health Ministry is one of resilience, dedication, and unwavering commitment—an extraordinary symphony conducted amidst the storm.

Some of the important key areas where the involvement, guidance, and direction of the judiciary was observed, while approaching to vaccinate the largest population by country-size, are as follows:

1. *Policy Review & Vaccination in Phased Manner*: The phased administration of Covid-19 vaccination was implemented to prioritize vulnerable populations, such as healthcare workers, elderly individuals, and those with comorbidities, based on risk factors and available vaccine supply. The judiciary reviewed the rationale behind the phased vaccination plan, assessed its scientific basis, and

considered the constitutional and legal aspects involved. Hon'ble Courts also evaluated whether the phased approach is reasonable, non-discriminatory, and in line with public health objectives.

The Honorable Supreme Court in *Re: Distribution of Essential Supplies & Services during Pandemic* case observed that Union of India has sufficiently clarified that the prioritization of the population for Covid-19 vaccination in phases 1 and 2 was as per the global best practices and was the best strategy. This strategy to vaccinate healthcare workers, frontline workers, and persons above the age of 45 years with comorbidity was rationale and sound in nature. It was noted that these demographic groups were at a heightened risk of infection and mortality of Covid-19 virus, necessitating their free and prioritized vaccination by the Government. This also ensured that healthcare workers like doctors, nurses, paramedics frontline workers like police, sanitary workers, and others who were designated as frontline workers were protected from the disease and thus were able to regularly perform their duty during pandemic.

2. *Vaccine Mandates and Legal Challenges:* This topic of vaccine mandate was the main contention in the case of *Jacob Puliyel v. Union of India and others* in the Hon'ble Supreme Court of India. During pandemic, the government was trying its best to use all the available strategies to limit the spread of the disease. It was always made clear by the central government that vaccination was voluntary; however, it was expected that the public will raise to the occasion and get themselves vaccinated.

   However, the speed of spread of pandemic in certain geographic areas was very high. During these unprecedented times, in some cases, the state governments, cities, corporations, and institutes implemented vaccine mandates or vaccination requirements for certain activities or sectors.

   There were legal challenges raised against such mandates. In *Jacob Puliyel v. Union of India and others*, before the Hon'ble Supreme Court of India, the Petitioner urged the Court to direct the Central Government to immediately repeal all orders, notifications, and instructions of mandatory vaccination because they were arbitrary and capricious, and not based on medical expertise or scientific consensus. It was also contended that mandatory enforcing Covid-19 vaccination could violate individuals' right to make informed choices and personal autonomy, safeguarded by Article 21 of the Constitution of India as a fundamental right. Further, that the mandatory vaccination measures deprive individuals of their Constitutional right to personal autonomy. Petitioner further contended that the vaccine mandates, wherein imposition of certain restrictions like prohibition on movement and access to welfare schemes on unvaccinated individuals could be deemed ultra-virus to the Constitution.

   The petitioner also emphasized that natural immunity acquired after recovering from Covid-19 is stronger and more enduring than vaccine-induced immunity. They further underscored that current vaccines are ineffective against variants, meaning both vaccinated and unvaccinated individuals can still spread the virus.

The Union of India, along with several state governments, contradicted the aforementioned arguments by asserting that vaccines have been demonstrated to be safe and effective. Additionally, they highlighted that emergency authorizations of vaccines, along with associated clinical trials, are conducted within the legal framework of the country. The government argued that any further debate on this matter could exacerbate existing vaccine hesitancy in the nation.

The Union of India argued that executive decision were taken based on national and global scientific and health expert opinions, especially concerning critical public health issues like the Covid-19 pandemic, restrictions and prohibition on movement, appropriate social behavior, and vaccination in the country. Further, the Constitution of India provides the State with the power to enact legislation for the preservation of Public Health, including the power to regulate and control matters relating to the prevention and control of diseases, their transmission, entry, and spread within its jurisdiction. It was further contended that in unprecedented times of Covid-19 pandemic, the need to protect population surpassed the individual's right to remain unvaccinated. In addition to its argument, the Union of India also submitted several orders/judgments of the Hon'ble Supreme Court of India and the Hon'ble High Courts, as well as those from the higher courts of the United States of America and New Zealand.

The petitioner opposed the position of the Union of India, asserting that the Hon'ble Supreme Court of India is obligated to protect the fundamental rights of individuals, necessitating a judicial scrutiny, especially in uncertain times. The petitioner side supported their arguments with precedents from the Supreme Court of India, demonstrating that executive/administrative policy decisions can be subject to judicial review if they are manifestly arbitrary or unreasonable, and/or violates the fundamental/constitutional rights of the citizens.

The Supreme Court recognized the fact that the virus is evolving over the time and changing its pace and intensity. Based on scientific evidences and data available, from the WHO and other global and national agencies, it supported the vaccination efforts by the Government of India as necessary in the interest of public health and safety. The Supreme Court re-emphasized that there will be conflicting scientific evidence on every issue; however, the role of policymaking remains exclusively with the executive. However, the judiciary still retains jurisdiction to assess whether the implemented policy aligns with standards of fairness, avoids manifest arbitrariness, and upholds the right to life and personal liberty of all individuals. Accordingly, the Honorable Supreme Court held that, the executive if the situation arises again may take a decision to enforce vaccine mandates; however, that nothing prevents the judiciary from re-examining the issues of fundamental rights as raised by the petitioner. However, at that point of time when the judgement was passed, since the pandemic had eased out, the government should remove all the vaccine mandates.

3. *Emergency Approval of Covid-19 Vaccines:* The emergency approval process for vaccines involves regulatory authorities granting authorization on a fast track mode. In cases where concerns were raised about the adequacy of the approval process or the safety and efficacy of a particular vaccine, the courts

examined the decision-making process of regulatory bodies, assessed compliance with legal standards, and provide directions or recommendations as necessary.

The Hon'ble Supreme Court in *Jacob Puliyel v. Union of India and others* also observed that "on the basis of substantial material filed before this Court reflecting the near-unanimous views of experts on the benefits of vaccination in addressing severe disease from the infection, reduction in oxygen requirement, hospital and ICU admissions, mortality and stopping new variants from emerging, this Court is satisfied that the current vaccination policy of the Union of India is informed by relevant considerations and cannot be said to be unreasonable or manifestly arbitrary.

4. *Publication of Clinical Trial Data of Vaccines:* The judiciary examined claims/arguments from various stakeholders, including vaccine manufacturers, regulatory bodies, and public health experts, to determine the balance between public interest, scientific knowledge, and intellectual property rights. The courts also provided directions or guidelines to ensure transparency in the publication of clinical trial data, particularly regarding vaccine safety, efficacy, adverse events, and other relevant information.

   In the *Jacob Puliyel* case, the petitioner argued that clinical trial data for Covaxin and Covishield vaccine has not been publicly disclosed by the Government of India. They emphasized the importance of releasing this raw data to assess potential adverse events across different age groups and populations, allowing individuals to make informed decisions about vaccination. In response, the Union of India specified that emergency use approvals were granted to Covaxin and Covishield following proper procedures under Drug Regulation in India. All relevant experts and bodies were consulted and scientific evidences were collected before granting these emergency use approvals.

   The Hon'ble Supreme Court acknowledged the rigorous statutory requirements for vaccine manufacturers and participants in clinical trials process. It disagreed with the petitioner's claim that emergency vaccine approvals were granted in haste.

5. *Deliberations of Expert Bodies:* The judiciary also assessed the transparency, fairness, and legality of the decision-making processes followed by these expert bodies like NTAGI, NEGVAC, and National AEFI Committee. They also examined the considerations of public health, safety, efficacy, and equity were adequately addressed in their deliberations.

   The Hon'ble Supreme Court in *Jacob Puliyel v. Union of India and others* case also noted that "the material provided by the Union of India, do not warrant the conclusion that restricted emergency use approval had been granted to Covishield and Covaxin in haste, without thorough review of the relevant data. The court also noted that relevant information relating to these meetings are available in public domain and therefore, challenge to the procedures adopted by the expert bodies while granting regulatory approval to the vaccines on the ground of lack of transparency cannot be entertained".

6. *Vaccine Pricing and Procurement:* In the initial stages of vaccination, the responsibility of procuring and distribution of Covid-19 vaccine was taken care by the Union of India. As the production of Covid-19 vaccine stabilized, it was felt that state government and the private sector should also take responsibility for procuring the Covid-19 vaccine. This led to the "Liberalized Vaccination Policy". This policy had provision for state government and private sector to procure 50% of the total doses of the produced quantity of Covid-19 vaccine. However, the manufacturers offered different prices for the Government of India and the state government and private providers. The price of vaccine for Union Government were the lowest. Introduction of this new liberalized policy led to a flux of new court cases where the main prayer was about the difference in the price of the same vaccine for central government and others.

   The Hon'ble Supreme Court of India also took note of this and examined issue of differential pricing of vaccines and the government's role in ensuring affordable access to vaccines. The Amici appointed by the Hon'ble Supreme Court have pointed out that many State/UT Governments and local municipal bodies have issued tenders and attempted negotiations with manufacturers, but have largely been unsuccessful, as manufacturers prefer negotiating with central governments rather than separate State/UT Governments. Furthermore, it was observed that the Central Government is better positioned to utilize its purchasing powers and sovereign authority to negotiate for larger quantities of vaccines at reasonable prices. This observation by the Hon'ble Supreme Court of India led to a course correction, where the Union of India again took the entire responsibility of procurement and distribution of vaccine to all states for free vaccination in the Government Covid-19 Vaccination Centers. This has shown that the proactive nature of the judiciary and the flexible nature of the government ensured, Team Health India delivering more than 220 core doses of Covid-19 vaccine in a record time.
7. *Supply of Adequate Quantity of Vaccines:* During the initial days of the pandemic, there was a constant demand for extra dose of vaccine by various states. Vaccine being biological and its production being a time taking process, limits the number of doses which can be produced. It was a fact that the targeted population of the country was huge and vaccine eagerness was seen throughout the pandemic, the Union of India had taken a policy of equitable distribution of vaccine. This meant that the finite quantity of vaccine which was available at any point of time was distributed across all the states based on the population percentage of that state in respect to the population of the country. This ensured that any big state should not predate on the vaccine need of a small state or union territory. Multiple court cases were filed to ensure that extra doses of Covid-19 vaccines were made available over and above the doses supplied to these states. However, the Union of India had always maintained their policy of equitable distribution and never deviated from it.
8. *Digital Divide:* For Covid-19 vaccination, it was a conscious decision to do all the vaccination though the COWIN Portal. In doing so, the government had considered the need to person who did not have any access to internet facility or

were unable to do navigate the COWIN portal. Despite this many court cases were registered regarding the provisions made for ensuring that those who have limited computer skills or those who do not have access to internet. The policies of the government and the facilities were brought to the notice of the Hon'ble courts and the courts were satisfied.

9. *Data Collection and Reporting:* The Courts emphasized the importance of accurate and transparent data collection and reporting in the vaccination program. Hon'ble Courts directed the government to provide regular updates on vaccination coverage, doses administered, and other relevant data.
10. In the initial stages of vaccination, the responsibility of procuring and distribution of Covid-19 vaccine was taken care by the Union of India. As the production of Covid-19 vaccine stabilized, it was felt that state government and the private sector should also take responsibility for procuring and giving Covid-19 vaccine. This led to the implementation of The Liberalized Vaccination Policy. This policy had provision for state government and private sector to procure 50% of the total doses of the produced quantity of Covid-19 vaccine. However, there was a difference in the prices of Covid-19 vaccine for the Government of India and the state government and private providers. The price of vaccine for Union Government, state and private providers were all different with the price for the Union Government being the lowest, followed by that for state government and vaccine for private providers were the highest. Introduction of this new liberalized policy led to a flux of new court cases where the main prayer was about the difference in the price of the same vaccine for central government and state government. The Hon'ble Supreme Court of India also took note of this issue.

    This observation by the Hon'ble Supreme Court of India led to a course correction, where the Union of India again took the entire responsibility of procurement and distribution of vaccine to all states for free vaccination in the Government Covid-19 Vaccination Centers. This has shown that the proactive nature of the judiciary and the flexible nature of the government ensured, MoHFW delivering more than 220 core doses of Covid-19 vaccine in a record.
11. *Correction/Modification of Vaccination Certificates:* Certain individuals encountered errors or corrections/modifications were required in their vaccination certificates as per need of the hour. To address those challenges, public interest petitions or other legal remedies were initiated to address their concerns and request the correction or modification of their vaccination certificates.

    One of the most critical cases in this regard was filed by Mr. Narendra Kumar Das and Ms. Tulasi Swain in the Hon'ble Orissa High Court. The petitioners claimed that they have received two doses of the vaccines at a private Covid-19 Vaccination Center on March 1 and April 1, 2021. However, the dates and name of vaccination center are mentioned incorrectly in the Covid-19 final vaccination certificates.

    As per the direction dated 03.03.2022 of the Hon'ble Orissa High Court, the Ministry of Health, and Family Welfare (MoHFW) started the utility for correction of date on vaccination certificates through Co-WIN portal. The Hon'ble

Orissa High Court directed the MoHFW to adequately advertise the availability of the Covid-19 vaccination certificate correction utility on Co-WIN.

The Hon'ble Orissa High Court in order dated 03.03.2022 directed the Union of India to:

- Provide corrected vaccination certificate.
- Come up with concrete suggestions for correcting the dates on the Covid-19 certificates, after the proof of the same has been provided by any individual.

It was submitted by Union of India that facility for change in vaccination date, vaccine type, and vaccination center cannot be given at beneficiary level because it is critical information during vaccination process. This information can only be authenticated by concerned vaccination center or administrative authority, under which such vaccinations have been conducted. Further, if such utility is to be provided to beneficiary level it will be against program guidelines since the dose interval between any two doses (i.e., first dose and second dose, second dose and precaution dose) have been scientifically fixed by technical expert group and if this is allowed, it may be harmful to beneficiary as this facility can be misused for taking undue advantages by changing critical information by tampering the data on vaccination process.

However, there may be some genuine instances for change in such critical information. Therefore, in the compliance affidavit, it was submitted to the Hon'ble High Court of Orissa that change of such information is only allowed at the level of district immunization officer. Beneficiary can apply for change of such information (vaccination date, vaccine type, and vaccination center) submitting adequate proofs supporting the claim for such change on the Co-WIN Portal. District Immunization Officer will ascertain the facts of such application and would resolve and settle the claim accordingly.

12. *Implementation of Booster Dose:* Public interest litigations (PILs) were filed challenging or seeking guidance on the implementation of booster doses to the entire adult population or a certain class of population in the country. The Honorable courts evaluated the scientific evidence, expert recommendations, and government policies regarding booster doses and provided appropriate directions to the government in this regard.
13. *Vaccination in Residential Societies:* Due to vaccine eagerness and the Covid-19 vaccination centers experienced huge crowd, many court cases were registered with a plea to have vaccination centers near to their houses. Taking cognizance of the need and demand of the citizens, the Near to Home Vaccination Policy was framed and implemented. Under this policy, a provision was made for arranging Covid-19 vaccination camp in the Residential Societies provided adequate space was made available for vaccination as per the Covid-19 operational guidelines.
14. *Vaccination at Workplaces:* Certain court cases were filed where the citizens argued that due to work it becomes difficult for them to go to the Covid-19 vaccination centers and get vaccinated. It was requested that the vaccination services may be provided in their office premises. This request was taken into

consideration and the guidelines for Workplace Vaccination were framed and issued. The government allowed workplaces to send their request, and organized vaccination camps within their own walls, harmonizing work with wellness.

15. *Vaccination of Homeless, Disabled and Bedridden People, Care Givers of Disabled, and Person Without Identity Card:* The National Covid-19 Vaccination Programme had inbuilt provision for ensuring that all the abovementioned groups were provided with free vaccination. However, many court cases were filed to ensure that these groups had access to vaccine. The Hon'ble Courts were informed about the same. One case for vaccination of person with disabilities was also filed in the Hon'ble Supreme Court of India. The Hon'ble court instructed the Union government to take inputs from the Ministry of Social Justice, specifically the Department of Person with Disabilities to make the Covid-19 vaccination process more inclusive. As instructed, the comments from the Ministry of Social Justice were received and all the suggestions were incorporated in the program. One of the strong demands in many court cases were to make the provision for vaccination for bedridden person to be given at home, as bedridden persons were not able to move and come to the nearest vaccination center and that these bedridden people were more vulnerable to Covid-19 infection. These demands were taken into consideration and the Government of India launched the "Har Ghar Dastak Campaign." Under this program, mobile teams were formed and sent to houses of all who have missed vaccine, especially identifying individuals who were disabled, bedridden including care givers of the disabled person so that the no one is left out from the net of vaccination.
16. *Reporting and Evaluation of Adverse Events Following Immunization System:* The courts played a significant role in examining the functioning and effectiveness of the AEFI reporting and evaluation system of Covid-19 vaccination and issued appropriate directions to strengthen the system across the country. The Hororable courts considered many factors such as the quality of data collection, the scope and comprehensiveness of adverse event reporting, the involvement of healthcare professionals in the evaluation process, and the actions taken by regulatory bodies and healthcare authorities based on AEFI reports.

    The petitioner in the *Jacob Puliyel v. Union of India and others* case argued that there have been numerous instances of adverse events and fatalities following vaccination, and the government lacked a suitable mechanism for reporting such incidents.

    The Union of India argued that they conscientiously obey the procedures and protocols outlined in the National Adverse Event Following Immunization (AEFI) Surveillance Guidelines and WHO guidelines for monitoring adverse events after immunization. Moreover, it was submitted that the COWIN SAFE-VAC portal has been operationalized for reporting of all adverse events following immunization (AEFIs) by the District Immunization Officers, doctors from private institutions and other stakeholders. Serious and severe AEFI cases, including reported deaths and hospitalization, undergo rapid review and analysis. Causality assessment of such cases is conducted by a team of trained subject experts on priority bases.

The Honorable Supreme Court in *Jacob Puliyel v. Union of India and others* (Jacob Puliyel v Union of India and others, 2022) cases observed that "there exists a well-defined mechanism for collection of data, relating to adverse events that occur due to covid-19 vaccines." Thus, the Honorable Supreme Court rejected the petitioner's challenge to the existing AEFI mechanism but stressed on the importance of reporting adverse and suspected adverse events. The Honorable Supreme Court the Union of India to enable and create a system for individuals and private medical practitioners to report such events.

17. *Vaccine Side Effects and Compensation:* The Honorable courts have shown concerns about adverse events following immunization (AEFI) and the need for an efficient mechanism to address compensation claims.
18. *Photo of Prime Minister of India in Covid-19 Vaccination Certificate:* Many court cases filed in the form of Public Interest Litigations in the hon'ble High Courts and Supreme Court of India. One such case deserve attention. In the Hon'ble Kerala High Court, one petition was filed, seeking objection to the photo of the Hon'ble Prime minister of India on the Covid-19 vaccination certificate. The petitioner stated that the photograph of Hon'ble Prime Minister of India on the Covid-19 certificate was a violation of his fundamental right. The case was decided in favor of the government and the Hon'ble High Court also imposed a penalty on the litigant for having such filovirus case and wasting the time of the Judiciary.
19. *Using Public Interest Litigation as a Way of Getting Information:* One court case in Hon'ble Delhi High Court was filed as a Public Interest litigation and the litigant wanted to get some data on the Covid-19 vaccination. The Hon'ble court took critical note of the case and dismissed the PIL with a warning that the route of PIL should not be taken lightly as the information sought could have been got by using the facility of Right to Information Act. The Hon'ble Court also imposed a penalty on the litigant for wasting the time of judiciary.
20. *Vaccination of Migrants and Nepali Workers in India:* The matter of Covid-19 vaccination of immigrants and Nepali laborers in Uttarakhand were taken up as PIL in Hon'ble High Court of Rajasthan and Uttarakhand, respectively. On both cases, the Hon'ble Courts ensured that these groups of individuals indeed received the Covid-19 vaccine.
21. *Salary of Schoolteacher Withheld:* One case was registered in the Hon'ble Delhi High Court where one schoolteacher approached the court for getting his salary. The petitioner argued that he had a medical condition and was advised by his doctor for not getting the Covid-19 vaccine. The school in its enthusiasm to have 100% Covid-19 vaccination withheld the salary for want of Covid-19 vaccination. This case was resolved in favor of the petitioner since the Hon'ble Supreme court in the Jacob Pulliyel case had asked to remove vaccine mandate.
22. *Early Booster Dose for International Travel:* Having a certificate of booster dose was essential for any international travel. India had its own booster dose policy where the booster dose was provided after 9 months of completion of the

second dose of the primary vaccination. However, many European countries were giving a booster dose at 6 months interval and thus many students, athletes, sick person needing international travel for treatment purpose, business groups, and government officials were unable to undertake the international travel on time. Taking note of this scenario, it was decided to reduce the duration of giving booster dose to these specific groups at an interval of 6 months to facilitate their travel.

7.1 Conclusion

To conclude, the judicial realm played an animated role in scrutinizing and reshaping the vaccination policy, orchestrating a symphony of directives to guide the government.

While vaccination remained a voluntary choice, an expectant hope lingered that the populace would rally in the fight against the pandemic. The Honorable courts, acknowledging personal autonomy enshrined under Article 21, but also recognized that public health considerations could warrant specific actions if the data supported such measures.

As concerns resonated about the thoroughness of the vaccine approval process and the safety and effectiveness of certain vaccines, the courts scrutinized regulatory decisions considering the complex choreography behind the authorization. The judiciary's discerning eye inspected the warp and weft of decisions taken by expert bodies and concluded that the very fabric of the decision-making process was not woven with haste.

The Honorable Courts directed the Union of India's participation, urging them to re-evaluate the Liberalized Vaccination Policy's facets to ensure equitable distribution and effective mitigation.

The judiciary reviewed the logic and constitutionality of the phased vaccination plan. The Honorable Courts recognized the rationale in prioritizing healthcare workers, frontline warriors, and those with comorbidities. The resonance of demand of easy access led to the harmonious creation of the Near to Home Vaccination Policy. Similarly, on the plea of convenience of vaccinating in the office space, the MoHFW issued Guideline for Workplace Vaccination. As the vaccination journey unfolded, the vulnerable, the homeless, disabled, and those without identity cards sought the legal symphony's intervention to secure their vaccination rights. The heartrending plea of bedridden individuals echoed, for vaccination at home. In response, the government composed a unique melody, the "Har Ghar Dastak" campaign.

Responding to a petition MoHFW while balancing the need for corrections in vaccination certificate with potential misuse, outlined a careful process of allowing change at the level of the district immunization officer.

In the legal ensemble, the migrants and Nepali workers got included into the vaccination narrative. As international borders beckoned, the courts interwove the duration of booster doses to facilitate seamless international travel.

As the curtain falls on this extraordinary chapter, the stage remains set for India's vaccination odyssey. A tale where the Union of India's resolve, met by the courts' vigilant oversight, led to the delivery of over 220 crore vaccine doses in record time. The symphony of governance and justice, attuned to the nation's needs, transcended challenges, and propelled India toward its vaccination pinnacle.

Planning for Human Resource and Their Capacity Building Under National Covid-19 Vaccination Program

8

Veena Dhawan and Palak Badhwar

Abstract

This chapter explores the critical role of a skilled and well-trained health workforce in the successful implementation of India's National Covid-19 Vaccination Program. The program, first of its kind, utilized a diverse range of personnel, including healthcare workers, program managers, and volunteers, ensuring the efficient delivery of vaccination services across the nation. Mixed training methods were adapted to the scale of the program, utilizing both in-person and virtual platforms due to the pandemic's constraints, for disseminating knowledge to over a million health manpower personnel. The trainings covered a range of areas from vaccination procedures, adverse event management, and technology use to community engagement. In addition, India shared its experiences with 13 countries, fostering global cooperation. The success of the program underscores the importance of dynamic training approaches, inter-sectoral collaboration, and a well-prepared workforce in overcoming public health challenges, ensuring effective vaccination coverage and fostering international solidarity in combating the pandemic.

Keywords

Hybrid training · Training · Capacity building · Public health workforce · Virtual training · Quality training · Skilled workforce

V. Dhawan (✉)
MoHFW, New Delhi, India

P. Badhwar
UNDP, New Delhi, India

M. Agnani et al. (eds.), *India's Covid-19 Vaccine Drive*,
https://doi.org/10.1007/978-981-95-8138-2_8

The health workforce has crucial role to play in implementation of every program, and it is the skilled, well-trained workforce that drives success and ensures delivery of quality services and program's sustainability. The Immunization Programme of India engages a variety of workforce for various functions to be carried out. It includes program managers, medical officers, supervisors, data entry operators, cold chain handlers, auxiliary nurse midwives (ANM/GNM), and accredited social health activists (ASHA).

Like other programs, for immunization too the planning, policies making and workflow are defined at the national and state level. While the human resources at the grass root level execute the assigned task, using their skill to ensure successful policies and workflow.

In our country, most of the health programs operate under the umbrella of National Health Mission (NHM) which supports the necessary training to human resources for health. For the National Covid-19 Vaccination Program, the available human resources under NHM, such as ANMs, GNMs, and ASHAs, were trained to meet the program's requirements. The country's public health system is supported roughly by 3 lakh ANMs and 10 lakh ASHAs, who served as vaccinators and mobilizers, respectively. Recognizing the immense scale of the program, additional human resources were by the state based on their education, skill set, and suitability for specific roles to ensure a swift and efficient implementation of the program.

Trainings under the Universal Immunization Programme have been conducted for the same cadre of functionaries and ground-level implementers for introduction of any new vaccine and scale-up of existing vaccines. Still it was a challenge to train the health work force under National Covid-19 Vaccination Program, as the target beneficiaries were different. This time, adults across all age groups as per the scientific prioritization, including those with comorbidities, were to be inoculated, expanding the existing experience of inoculating children and pregnant women. The vaccinators being the first point of contact for the citizens desiring information about the vaccination, its safety and efficacy, there was a need to train them effectively to address the queries and apprehensions of the citizens. Hence, the quality of trainings could not be compromised at any cost. Each training focused on the five-member vaccination team to be formed with specific roles at each vaccination site, protocols to be followed for those vaccination sites which were other than the health institutions and the process of providing the vaccination services starting from registration of each beneficiary on Co-WIN application following identity verification, vaccination, and monitoring for any adverse effects following the vaccination.

In view of the scale of the vaccination program, private sector was also included and trained along with the cadre of inter-sectoral or allied health organizations such as Ministry of Defence, Railway, and ESIC. The human resource belonging to the private sector was trained in two rounds through the web-cast mode for 1000 participants each.

Further, in the past, most trainings were conducted in-person, using traditional classroom platforms. However, due to social distancing requirements and the ongoing spread of the virus, it became necessary to explore alternative methods to train many human resources. As a result, a hybrid training model was adopted.

Based on the lessons learned from the expansion of the Pneumococcal Conjugate Vaccine (PCV) in Uttar Pradesh and Goa, along with the Sub-National Immunization Days (SNID) of Polio vaccination in September 2020, it was realized that State training of trainers (ToTs) could be conducted effectively using virtual platforms. For the cascade of training at the district and sub-district levels, a combination of face-to-face and virtual training modalities was deemed appropriate.

As a result, a significant portion of the trainings were conducted virtually, utilizing online platforms such as the National Informatics Centre (NIC), Webex, Google Meet, Microsoft Teams, ECHO-India, and other State/UT specific platforms up to the district level. However, at the sub-district level and below, especially in areas with limited internet availability and the need to develop hands-on skill, traditional classroom training was used. These in-person sessions were conducted in well-ventilated venues in a group of 15–20 trainees, while adhering to social distancing and Covid-19 appropriate behavior norms, including hand hygiene, mandatory mask usage, and maintaining a physical distance of 2 gaz between participants.

All modules of virtual or classroom training were developed at the national level. These were tailored to the needs of the target audience and accordingly a training plan, defining the target audience at all levels under various thematic areas, was also formulated.

While maintaining the quality of these virtual trainings, several measures were adopted to ensure the security for these trainings. These measures included pre-registration of participants, requiring passwords for entry, and using virtual waiting rooms to verify the identity of intended participants before granting them access to the training sessions. Nonetheless, the training material and modules were shared through the mode of webcast or web-link, depending on the type of training and sensitivity of the discussion.

Additionally, a blended approach of self-learning modules and facilitated training or just self-learning training modules complementing the instructor-led trainings were hosted on the following for easy reference at any given time:

- Government Online Training Portal, i.e., iGOT on Ministry of Human Resource and Development's DIKSHA platform
- Raid Immunization Skill Enhancement (RISE) platform

The virtual platforms used for capacity building and sharing experiences in the Covid-19 vaccination program played a crucial role in providing a comprehensive knowledge and skill-building package. These platforms acted as valuable supplements to the standard classroom trainings by offering various interactive tools such as videos, power point presentations, and other training materials.

By utilizing these virtual platforms, both regular and refresher trainings were conducted efficiently based on the specific needs of the participants. The interactive nature of these sessions allowed for better engagement and enhanced understanding of the subject matter.

These online resources and training materials were accessible to a wider audience, enabling individuals from different locations to benefit from the knowledge and expertise shared by India. They served as valuable tools in strengthening the capabilities of vaccination teams and enhancing their readiness to tackle challenges effectively.

Overall, the use of virtual platforms as a knowledge and skill-building package complemented traditional classroom trainings, facilitating continuous learning and skill enhancement in the Covid-19 vaccination program.

In all the mentioned modalities, it was ensured that the quality of the training remained consistent. The training sessions adhered to the National Covid-19 Vaccination Guidelines and were later adapted to suit the specific needs of each State/Union Territory and the target audience. To maintain an effective learning environment, all trainings, whether virtual or in-classroom, were organized in small batches, typically comprising 15–20 participants at the sub-district level. This allowed for personalized attention and better interaction between trainers and trainees. The understanding and comprehension of the trainees were continuously monitored during the training using pre-defined key indicators. This monitoring process helped identify any areas of difficulty or gaps in understanding, allowing trainers to address these issues promptly. The training content was presented using well-structured PowerPoint presentations, instructive videos, role-plays, exercises, and interactive discussions. These diverse training methods catered to different learning styles and ensured a comprehensive understanding of the subject matter. By combining various engaging and informative techniques, the training sessions successfully conveyed important information and equipped the human resources with the necessary skills and knowledge to carry out their roles effectively in the National Covid-19 Vaccination Program.

A vaccination team composed of five members was designated to provide vaccination services to the eligible population, and each member had specific roles and responsibilities as follows:

Vaccination Officer 1 This individual was responsible for checking the registration status of beneficiaries and verifying their identity with photo ID proof. The Vaccination Officer 1 could be personnel from various entities such as Police guards, Civil Defense Officers, National Cadet Corps (NCC) members, National Service Scheme (NSS) volunteers, or Nehru Yuva Kendra Sangathan (NYKS) volunteers.

Vaccination Officer 2 The role of Vaccination Officer 2 involved authenticating or verifying the beneficiary's appointment and registering unregistered beneficiaries on the Co-WIN system. This could be a representative from the Health Department, Integrated Child Development Services (ICDS), or other Government Departments (e.g., election model).

Vaccination Officers 3 and 4 These officers were responsible for crowd management, guiding non-registered beneficiaries, ensuring each beneficiary's 30-min waiting time after receiving the vaccine dose, and monitoring for any adverse event symptoms following vaccination. The team members from Information, Education, and Communication (IEC)/communication departments or other Government Departments were assigned to these roles.

Vaccinator The Vaccinator's primary duty was to administer the vaccine to the citizens. They were also responsible for accurately recording and reporting each vaccination event in the Co-WIN system. Additionally, the Vaccinator was required to provide the citizen with four key messages regarding vaccination: details about the vaccine received and the disease it prevents, the schedule for the next vaccine dose, information about possible minor adverse events and how to manage or report them, and guidance on accessing the vaccination certificate.

In addition to the vaccination team members, a supervisor was designated to oversee three to five vaccination sites. The supervisor's responsibilities included ensuring sufficient vaccine availability and logistics at the sites and ensuring timely reporting of coverage and other relevant data.

By assigning specific roles and responsibilities to each team member, the vaccination process was streamlined and efficient, ensuring the smooth implementation of the vaccination program for the eligible population.

8.1 Identification of Additional Human Resources

Vaccinators Alongside the existing medical officers and auxiliary nurse midwives (ANM/GNM), the vaccination team included alternate vaccinators, such as doctors (MBBS, BDS, AYUSH), staff nurses (B.Sc. Nursing), MBBS and BDS interns, and pharmacists. These individuals received comprehensive training to safely handle the Covid-19 vaccine and administer it to the eligible population. They were considered credible and reliable sources of information regarding the new vaccine. The training covered various aspects, including vaccine details, dosage, interval, vaccine safety, possible adverse events, their management, safe injection practices, programmatic guidelines, and the usage of the Co-WIN (vaccinator module) system.

Mobilizers To enhance community engagement and promote vaccination, mobilizers were identified which included Self-Help Groups (SHGs), Non-Governmental Organizations (NGOs), Civil Society Organizations (CSOs), youth organizations, and the social mobilization network (Smnet) of UNICEF (which had previously been used for polio and Measles-Rubella campaign). These mobilizers were tasked with counseling and addressing any fears or misconceptions among the eligible population regarding vaccination. Their role was crucial in mobilizing and encouraging people to get vaccinated, ultimately contributing to the success of the vaccination program.

Capacity building for such a diverse group was a challenging task that demanded thorough planning and high-quality training delivered in an expedited manner within a compressed timeframe of 3–4 weeks. This contrasted with other vaccine introductions, where trainings could take 3–4 months to complete. The training initiative commenced on December 5, 2020, and was concluded on January 15, 2021, in a span of just 20 days.

Participants from various backgrounds had to be trained on the following key thematic areas:

1. Operational guidelines for Covid-19 vaccination and policies: Familiarizing participants with national vaccination program guidelines and policies.
2. Vaccination procedures and protocols: This covered the step-by-step process of administering vaccines, ensuring proper storage, and handling, and adhering to vaccination guidelines.
3. Vaccine safety and adverse event management: Participants were educated on recognizing and managing adverse events following immunization, ensuring the safety and well-being of vaccine recipients.
4. Technological aspects—Use of Co-Win Platform: Training on the utilization of the Co-WIN platform, including data entry, appointment scheduling, and managing vaccination records.
5. Communication and community engagement: Focus on effective communication strategies to dispel vaccine-related myths, address concerns, and encourage vaccine acceptance among the population. This also covered crisis communication for vaccine eagerness that was being observed in simultaneity to vaccine hesitancy. For addressing the concerns related to any adverse event following immunization (AEFI), an AEFI spokesperson in each agency/organization was identified and trained on factual communication in such cases.
6. Crowd management and logistics: Training on managing large crowds, organizing vaccination sites efficiently, and ensuring the availability of necessary resources.
7. Recording and reporting: Ensuring accurate and timely recording of vaccination data and reporting to appropriate authorities.

The extensive training on these thematic areas was vital in preparing the diverse group of vaccination teams to carry out their roles effectively and ensure the successful implementation of the National Covid-19 Vaccination Program.

The trainings on the key thematic areas were conducted in a cascaded manner, which included the following diverse individuals:

1. Operational guidelines for Covid-19 vaccination:

   At National Level: Principal Secretary (Health) and Mission Director (NHM) of all States, District Magistrate/District Collector of all Districts, State Programme Managers, Finance officers and other administrative officers, Municipal Commissioners, Urban Nodal Officers, State Senior Official, SEPIO, State Cold Chain Officers, State IEC officer, State data in-charge, Partners, National representatives of professional bodies such as IMA, IAP, AEFI Nodal officers, Defense Institutions.

At State/UT Level: Chief Medical Officer, District Immunization Officer, Urban Nodal Officers, Corporation Health Officer, District Programme Managers (NHM), District AEFI Nodal Officer, District Data manager, State IMA, IAP societies, Nodal officers of medical colleges, Other Departments including Supervisors, ICDS, Medical Colleges, Private practitioners.

At District Level: District Level Officers, Block Medical Officer, staff of Municipal Corporations, Nodal officers of Municipal health institutes, Block Programme Managers, staff of NUHM, Block Supervisors, Cold Chain Handlers, Data Entry Operators, District IAP societies, ICDS and other stake holders.

2. Use of Co-WIN platform: All level of officers from States/UTs, Central Health Institutes and other Nodal Ministries, Inter Ministerial Nodal Person.
3. Orientation Training on Dry Run for all States/UTs: Hon'ble Health Ministers of various states, Principal Secretary, Mission Director (NHM), State Immunization Officers, and District Immunization Officers of All States/UTs.
4. Orientation training of Helpline Agents on Co-WIN software for Covid-19 vaccine roll-out: States/UTs-1075/Covid-19 Call Centre, Medical Advice Helplines-104, Co-WIN technical helpline Call Centre and NHA Call Centre.
5. Media Orientation on Covid-19 Vaccination Program: Various media houses at the National and State/UT level, Regional Heads of PIB, Community Radio Networks, Social Media stakeholders.
6. Training on reporting of AEFI following Covid-19 vaccination: Nodal officers and Pharmacovigilance associates of 150 Adverse Drug Reaction (ADR) monitoring centers.
7. Media spokesperson on AEFI and other crisis situations for Covid-19 vaccinations: Mission Director (NHM), State Immunization Officers, States Media Spokespersons, State IEC Officers, AEFI Committee of all States/UTs.
8. Cold Chain Handling: Cold Chain Handler Module of Co-WIN and its corresponding part on eVIN was conducted at District level.
9. Alternate Vaccinators: Alternate Vaccinator Module of Co-WIN conducted at District level.
10. Social Mobilization: MAS, ASHA, AWW, SHGs, Civil Society Organizations (CSOs), Youth Groups like NCC, NSS and NYK, CBOs, PRIs at the Sub-District level.
11. Vaccinators: Training of ANMs and identified alternate vaccinators on Vaccinator Module of Co-WIN at Sub-District level.
12. Beneficiary Module: Surveyors and FLWs trained on the Beneficiary Module of Co-WIN for registering the eligible beneficiaries for Covid-19 vaccination.
13. Orientation on protocols to be followed for COVAXIN—Bharat Biotech Vaccine: State Immunization Officers of 12 States/UTs (initial introduction) with session sites to administer COVAXIN, namely, Delhi, Tamil Nadu, Maharashtra, Assam, Uttar Pradesh, Odisha, Bihar, Rajasthan, Telangana, Haryana, Karnataka, and Andhra Pradesh.
14. Doctors For You and La Pura Vida: Leveraging networks of doctors to address vaccine hesitancy among various communities.

To ensure the rapid implementation of the vaccination program in urban areas, a wide range of stakeholders and resources were engaged and oriented. This included urban officials, members of municipal corporations, urban local bodies, counselors, corporators, members of Resident Welfare Associations (RWAs), Mohalla Samitis, representatives of youth bodies, Mahila Aarogya Samiiti (MAS), Swachagrahis, and Self-Help Groups (SHGs).

In addition to the existing resources, such as Accredited Social Health Activists (ASHAs) and Anganwadi Workers (AWWs), these newly engaged stakeholders played a vital role in facilitating the vaccination program's effective execution in urban settings. Their active involvement and orientation ensured a comprehensive approach to reach and vaccinate the eligible population swiftly and efficiently in urban areas.

In fact, right on the day before the cascade of trainings had to begin, some of the leading officers of the program tested positive for Covid-19 and were under isolation as per the guidelines. Even then, the show went on without any glitch due to the well-designed and audience-specific modules. With the diligent efforts of the entire vaccination team, the timelines of trainings were strictly adhered to as planned.

During phase one of the vaccination program, approximately 75,000 Programme Officers/Medical Officers and 7,30,000 Health Workers got trained on different aspects of the vaccination program. In phase two, an additional 1,60,000 Frontline Workers received training to boost the vaccination efforts.

To ensure a robust workforce for vaccination, alternate vaccinators were identified. Over 2.64 lakh such identified vaccinators and 4.76 lakh other vaccination team officers underwent comprehensive training to effectively contribute to the vaccination process.

Furthermore, approximately 300 members of the National and State Adverse Events Following Immunization (AEFI) committees received specialized training on identifying and managing Adverse Events Following Immunization. This was critical in promptly addressing any adverse reactions that might occur after vaccination.

To optimize the usage of the technological component of the vaccination program, over 1 lakh users were trained on Co-WIN. This training equipped them with the necessary knowledge to effectively utilize the Co-WIN platform, a key tool in managing vaccination data and appointments.

From the beginning of the National Covid-19 Vaccination Program, a need was felt to create a platform for real-time dissemination of various updates related to vaccination program with a two-way communication to address the concerns of all States/UTs and to ensure clarity at all levels. All guidelines and orders were available on Ministry's website for easy access for all. Keeping this need in mind, orientation of the higher officials of States/UTs was conducted on regular basis, under the chairmanship of the Union Secretary (Health and Family Welfare) and Additional Secretary in charge of the National Covid-19 Vaccination Program. This arrangement illustrated the committed leadership at all levels ensuring the intensive scale-up of the vaccination program with zero turn-around time in implementation. Such extensive orientation and comprehensive training programs created a skilled and well-prepared workforce, which ensured the smooth implementation of the vaccination program to safeguard the health and well-being of the population.

In the spirit of Vasudhaiv Kutumbakam (world as one family), India demonstrated its commitment to global cooperation by extending support to other countries in their Covid-19 vaccination efforts. India conducted virtual training sessions to build capacity and share its experience of successfully rolling out the Covid-19 vaccine.

Thirteen countries, including Bahrain, Mauritius, Morocco, Oman, Seychelles, Brazil, Sri Lanka, Maldives, Bhutan, Mongolia, Nepal, Bangladesh, and Myanmar, participated in these training sessions. Officials from these countries actively engaged to learn from India's experiences, understand the mechanisms put in place for a successful vaccine rollout, and gain insights into implementation strategies that helped overcome various challenges.

The sharing of knowledge and experiences through these virtual trainings fostered collaboration and solidarity among nations in their fight against the pandemic. India's efforts in supporting other countries' vaccination programs were in line with the belief that the world is a global family, and collective action is essential to combat the Covid-19 pandemic effectively.

8.2 Conclusion

In the grand endeavor of India's National Covid-19 Vaccination Program, the strength of its health workforce proved to be pivotal. A diverse array of dedicated professionals, from program managers to grassroots workers, orchestrated a symphony of success. The meticulous planning, dynamic training methods, and innovative use of technology ensured the efficient execution of this monumental task. Virtual platforms enabled comprehensive training, reaching across geographical barriers and empowering a broad spectrum of individuals. Alternate vaccinators, mobilizers, and supervisors seamlessly blended into a cohesive vaccination team, each with a crucial role to play. Comprehensive training covered operational guidelines, vaccination procedures, safety, technology usage, communication, logistics, and reporting. The program's success extended beyond India's borders, as the nation generously shared its expertise through virtual training sessions with other countries. This global solidarity exemplified that collective effort can triumph over challenges. The National Covid-19 Vaccination Program stands as a testament to the power of a skilled, motivated, and well-trained health workforce in realizing a healthier and safer world for all.

Cold Chain Management for National Covid-19 Vaccination Programme

9

Mahesh Kumar Aggarwal

Abstract

Cold chain is a system of storing and transporting vaccines at the recommended temperatures from point of manufacturing to the point of use. It is an essential part of immunization supply chain which encompasses the planning, people, infrastructure, activities, MIS and resources to ensure last mile delivery of right vaccine at right place in right quantities. The country had experience of implementing UIP for childhood vaccinations for more than three and a half decade and had well established cold chain system and reliable and digitized immunization supply chain for the same. However, the media reports were sceptical regarding the availability of enough cold chain storage space and capacity to deliver the Covid-19 vaccines to the vaccination centres through the existing supply chain of UIP. Mindful of the requirements for impending nationwide Covid-19 vaccination program; the Government established the NEGVAC and subgroups to plan and guide. The concerned subgroup headed by a Union Secretary of Govt. was briefed about initial assessment of available cold chain storage space along with modalities of transporting the vaccines. The initial assessment revealed the adequacy of storage space to cater to 30 million doses. As directed by the sub-group, the cold chain space was planned to be augmented rapidly to accommodate for increased availability of Covid-19 vaccines later in shorter time. In view of this, it was decided to rapidly add more cold chain equipment to accommodate 300 million doses of Covid-19 vaccine. This was done through expediting the procurement at MoHFW level, through UNICEF supply, and through CSR funding from PSUs. The government took proactive steps to evaluate cold chain capacity and potential gaps, converting crisis into an opportunity for strengthen-

M. K. Aggarwal (✉)
Formerly at Ministry of Health & Family Welfare, Government of India,
New Delhi, India

M. Agnani et al. (eds.), *India's Covid-19 Vaccine Drive*,
https://doi.org/10.1007/978-981-95-8138-2_9

ing the system. This comprehensive approach, combining personnel expertise, established practices, and equipment reliability, was the key to success in executing the world's largest Covid-19 vaccination drive.

Keywords

Cold chain · Supply chain · ILR · Walk-in-cooler · UIP · NEGVAC · NCCVMRC UIP · Covid-19 vaccine

Earl Nightingale once said, "*All you need is the plan, the road map, and the courage to press on to your destination*". This wisdom rings true when we look at the incredible feat of India's National Covid-19 Vaccination Programme. The country successfully vaccinated its population with more than two billion doses in a short span of 2 years, by planning meticulously, following a clear roadmap, and showing remarkable determination.

To run any successful program, a good planning, well-designed implementation strategy, effective monitoring, mid-course correction and evaluation are critical components. Planning should consider what you have, in terms of people infrastructure and funds and how things will get done, where they need to be. It also needs to identify what's most important and also to set a timeline. Once a plan is finalized, it needs to put into action. This would include capacity building of human resources; strengthening and/or creation of supply chain for delivery of logistics in appropriate conditions and in right quantities at right place; creating demand for the services by devising appropriate communication strategies, managing financial, administrative and legal issues; developing mechanisms for inter-departmental, inter-sectoral coordination, etc. Then, a sound and efficient data management system, which could be digital, should be able to take care of monitoring, feedback, and mid-course corrections.

Vaccines are time- and temperature-sensitive products. Some of these are sensitive to heat, some to freezing and some to light. They need to be stored and transported at controlled temperatures according to product recommendations to maintain their efficacy. The expanding range of vaccines available necessitates a more effective and efficient operation of complex supply chain systems to ensure their safe delivery and storage. The introduction of new vaccines places greater demand on immunization supply chain logistics systems, as these vaccines tend to be more expensive, larger in volume, and less stable at different temperatures compared to traditional vaccines. The objective of the immunization supply chain is to optimize performance by ensuring availability, quality, and cost-effectiveness. This involves ensuring an adequate supply of vaccines for each immunization session, preventing temperature damage, and minimizing costs. Therefore, a well-functioning immunization supply chain acts as the backbone of any successful immunization programme.

Vaccines are biological products and may lose potency and degrade with each episode of exposure to temperatures below or above the recommended temperature range. Maintaining vaccines potency, right from the manufacturing facility to the administration of the vaccine to the beneficiary, requires a satisfactory cold chain system, maintaining the recommended temperature of storage, compliance to standards, and effective logistic management.

The essential components of immunization supply chain including cold chain system are as given in Fig. 9.1, and cold chain equipment used under Universal Immunization Programme in India are as shown in Fig. 9.2.

As mentioned earlier, efficient and effective planning is an important component of any successful programme for which assessment of existing resources provides the initial stepping stone. The subsequent section would give an understanding of existing resources before the start of Covid-19 vaccination campaign, along with public perception, media stories, how assessment was carried out and plans developed to further strengthen the system to meet out the needs of world' largest Covid-19 vaccination drive.

Were we prepared to receive, transport and store Covid-19 vaccine? Let us examine these questions by quoting, *Alexandria Ocasio-Cortez* in *Knock Down the House*: "*I am experienced enough to do this. I am knowledgeable enough to do this. I am prepared enough to do this. I am mature enough to do this. I am brave enough to do this.*"

So, Did, the country has the experience and knowledge? It is pertinent to know that the immunization programme in the country for the children was initiated as the 'Expanded Programme of Immunization' (EPI) by the Ministry of Health and Family Welfare (MoHFW), Government of India in 1978. In 1985, the programme evolved into the 'Universal Immunization Programme' (UIP). It was implemented in phases with the goal of covering all districts in the country by 1989–1990. Under UIP initially vaccines against six vaccine preventable diseases were available for administration to the children, namely, Childhood Tuberculosis, Diphtheria, Tetanus, Pertussis, Poliomyelitis and Measles. Over the years, many more vaccines

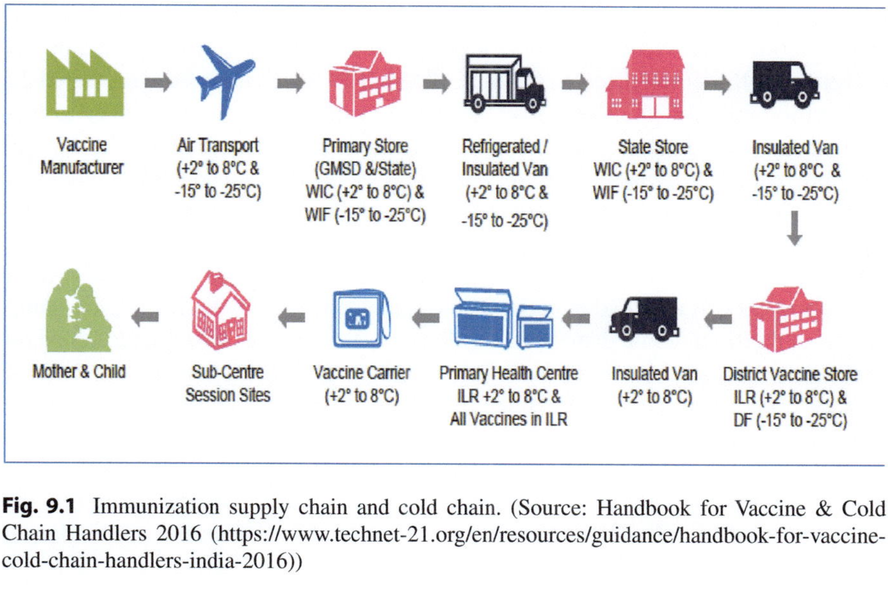

Fig. 9.1 Immunization supply chain and cold chain. (Source: Handbook for Vaccine & Cold Chain Handlers 2016 (https://www.technet-21.org/en/resources/guidance/handbook-for-vaccine-cold-chain-handlers-india-2016))

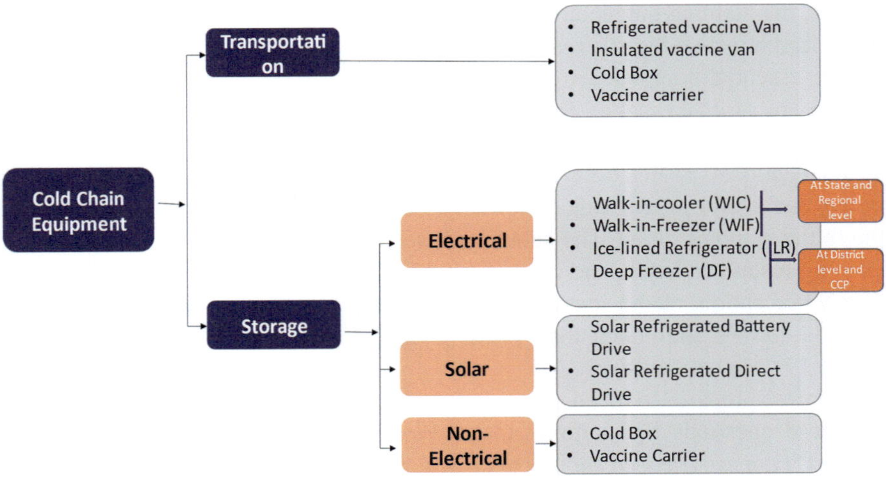

Fig. 9.2 Cold chain equipment used under UIP in India. (Source: Handbook for Vaccine & Cold Chain Handlers 2016 (https://www.technet-21.org/en/resources/guidance/handbook-for-vaccine-cold-chain-handlers-india-2016))

were added into the program and at present, and the vaccines are available against 12 vaccine preventable diseases. "The stated objectives of UIP were as follows:

- To rapidly increase immunization coverage
- To improve the quality of services
- To establish a reliable cold chain system to the health facility level
- Monitoring of performance"

As stated above, one of the objectives of the UIP relates to the establishment of reliable cold chain system up to the level of health facility. It was decided by the Government that Immunization division of MoHFW to be entrusted with Covid-19 vaccination drive, as Division had experience of running a well-established immunization program across all the States and UTs for delivering vaccines for 12 vaccine preventable diseases, with very effective and efficient cold chain network available up to primary health centres. UIP had experience of running Measles-Rubella campaign over a period of 2.5 years from February 2017 onwards covering around 350 million children in the age group of 9 months to 15 years across 34 States and UTs. It also had experience of conducting several JE vaccination campaigns in the JE endemic districts across several states in past two decades. Several phases of Intensified Immunization Drives against childhood vaccine preventable disease were also conducted since the launch of Mission Indradhanush in December 2014.

Previously UIP had experience of storing and transporting large number of vaccine doses through the cold chain system, which was in existence before the Covid-19 pandemic. It included large supplies of Oral Polio Vaccine (OPV) during the times of frequent mass scale campaigns of Pulse Polio Program since 1995.

Another important question to examine was "whether the country was prepared enough in terms of cold chain, to launch the Covid-19 vaccination campaign and carry it forward?" Though the country had experience and knowledge and existing cold chain network, it needed assessment in terms of numbers, to receive and store the quantities of the vaccine, which were likely to be available for Covid-19 vaccination program, in addition to the vaccines already needed to be stored for UIP. This assessment and subsequent timely actions would have decided if the country was prepared enough to launch the campaign.

Knowing well this need, even before the Covid-19 vaccines were made available, government started planning for efficient and effective rollout of National Covid-19 Vaccination Program. For this purpose, in August 2020 itself, Government of India constituted "National Expert Group on Covid-19 Administration" (NEGVAC) under Co-chairpersonships of Member (Health) NITI Aayog and Union Secretary, Health & Family Welfare. The other members of NEGVAC comprised of experts from scientific community, public health experts, Union Secretaries of important collaborating ministries like Pharmaceutical, External Affairs, Finance, IT and Principal Secretaries of Health and Family Welfare of four states. In its inaugural meeting on 12 August 2020, the National Expert Group on Vaccine Administration for Covid-19 (NEGVAC) discussed various options for delivery platforms, cold chain infrastructure and associated digital platforms for the rollout of Covid-19 vaccines. They also deliberated on the selection of Covid-19 vaccine candidates.

Simultaneously NEGVAC constituted a subgroup to assess the preparedness in terms of availability of cold chain infrastructure and related logistics like availability of syringes, etc. This subgroup was chaired by Union Secretary, Department of Pharmaceuticals. Subgroup through its regular meetings assessed, oversaw, monitored and provided valuable inputs not only to galvanize the existing infrastructure for delivery of the desired Covid-19 vaccination but also instructed and monitored for strengthening of cold chain infrastructure for enhanced requirements in view of likely increasing availability of Covid-19 vaccines and further inclusion of population into the eligibility criteria for vaccination. It would be pertinent to mention here that before and during the initial period of the Covid-19 vaccination campaign, there were frequent meetings of the subgroup, and by June 2021, it had conducted a total of 18 meetings.

Well before the launch of the Covid-19 vaccination drive, advisories were issued to the States/UTs and the Government Medical Stores Depots (GMSDs) for assessment of the existing total cold chain space, available additional cold chain space after accounting for the space requirements for the UIP vaccines, functional and non-functional cold chain equipment, and repair plan of the non-functional cold chain equipment. Multiple review meetings were conducted by the Immunization Division with states/UTs and GMSDs for assessing vaccine supply chain, providing guidance for taking appropriate actions to handle the high volume of the stocks including arrangement of storing spaces, transportation mechanism, capacity building of HRs, etc. These virtual interactive meetings with states/UTs continued almost on daily basis till the first billion doses were administered. Later on, these meetings were conducted on need based as the program had reached to auto pilot mode and required minimal guidance at least on cold chain front.

Cold chain network is the backbone of immunization program. Though UIP was in existence for nearly four decades, population perception about the quality, efficiency and sufficiency of existing transport and cold chain storage facilities under UIP and capacity of the government to rapidly strengthen the system further to carry forward the Covid-19 vaccination campaign was largely of scepticism and despair. Some of the quotes from media and experts are highlighted below to put the perspective in place.

> Covid-19: Vaccine production is not a problem for India, cold chain is. (Business Standard, 17 November 2020)

> *Covid-19 vaccine: How ready is India's supply chain?*—As India starts the second phase of its Covid-19 vaccine deployment, the question on the viability of its supply chain network, and its cold storage capability, has become more pertinent than ever (Fortune India: Business News, Strategy, Finance and Corporate Insight, 1 March 2021)

> India's Covid-19 Dilemma: Adults Need Vaccines, Supply Chains Geared for Children. (India Spend, 13 October 2020)

"*The entire existing cold chain capacity is inadequate for existing vaccination programs*" said T. Sundararaman, Coordinator of the People's Health Movement, an organization that works with academics and civil society. "*Your investment in cold chains needs to be to the order of five to 10 times what you're doing now. That level of cold equipment—to procure, to distribute, to allocate, to function, to train itself is a big undertaking.*" (Livemint n.d.) (India strengthening existing cold chain system for Covid-19 vaccination, dated: 23 November 2020)

It was not surprising that these kinds of doubts existed in the minds of people, public health experts and media despite having a very robust supply chain systems in place, which can be partly explained by the fact that the government seldom showcases or talks about what goes in preparation of a program, usually highlighting achievements only. However, Ministry of Health & family Welfare, Government of India, made efforts to reassure the people from time to time by issuing press releases and/or talking to media on preparedness issues including that of cold chain.

> The nation with the world's second-highest infections plans to use the existing cold chain network in place for its Universal Immunization Program, said Rajesh Bhushan, secretary to India's federal health ministry, in an email interview. (Business Standard n.d.)

"*An assessment of cold chain storage space has been carried out across the country for enhancement and augmentation for Covid-19 vaccine,*" Bhushan said in his email. "*Necessary actions have also been initiated to strengthen the existing cold chain system.*" (Livemint n.d.) (India strengthening existing cold chain system for Covid-19 vaccination, dated: 23 November 2020, accessed from https://www.livemint.com/news/world/india-strengthening-existing-cold-chain-system-for-covid-vaccination-11606129226560.html on 21/08/2023, p. 3).

Press Information Bureau of India releases were also helpful in reassuring the public at large regarding the preparation and commitment of the Government.

> The National Expert Group on Vaccine Administration of Covid-19 (NEGVAC) has recommended three prioritized population groups including Healthcare Workers (HCWs) (about 1 crore), Frontline Workers (FLWs) (about 2 crore), and Prioritized Age Group (about 27 crore). As vaccines are temperature sensitive and need to be stored in specific temperature, the present cold chain system consisting of 85,634 equipment for storage of vaccine at about 28,947 cold chain points across the country will be used for the cold chain administration. The current cold chain can store additional quantity of Covid-19 vaccine required for the first 3 Crore prioritized population i.e., Health Care Workers and Front-Line Workers. (PIB n.d.) (Central Government gears up for roll out of Covid-19 Vaccine-PIB, Govt of India, 25th December 2020)

As said earlier, the general perception was that existing cold chain capacity under UIP may be inadequate to cater to the extra load of Covid-19 vaccines. Doubts also existed around transportation of vaccines from manufacturers to the last cold chain point at PHC level and then to the vaccination centres. This kind of impressions were not unexpected as country was preparing for world's largest Covid-19 vaccination campaign. These impressions of inadequacy were further accentuated by various opinion leaders like freelancing public health experts who might have had limited understanding and exposure to the strengths of UIP and its field level realities and by industry experts especially those, who were concerned with cold chain transportation, equipment manufacturing and warehousing.

However, the fact was that UIP was existing for more than three and half decades and had experience of conducting many large-scale campaigns in specific age groups. There was an already existing immunization supply chain system including cold chain network across all the states/UTs. Figure 9.3 depicts vaccine and cold chain system which existed in 2020. There were more than 85,000 Ice-Lined Refrigerators (ILRs) and Deep Freezers (DFs), 240 Walk-in-Coolers (WICs), 70 Walk-in-Freezers (WIFs) across 28,932 cold chain points. Systems including HR,

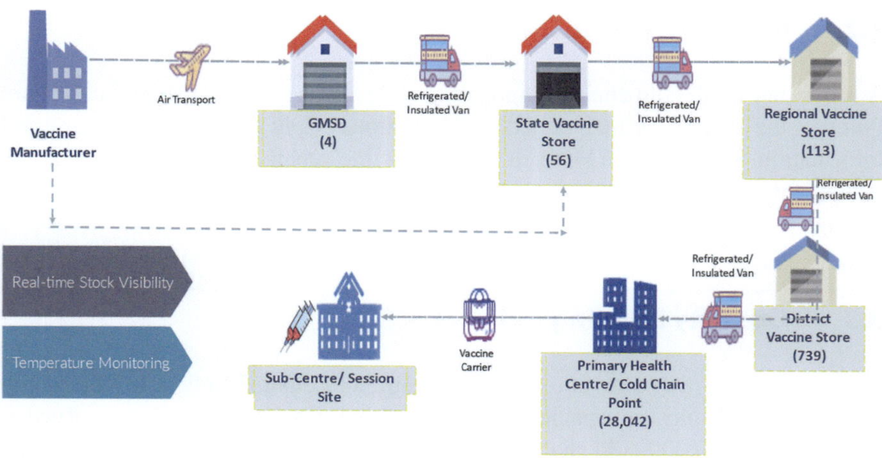

Fig. 9.3 Vaccine and cold chain system in 2020. (Source: Open-domain/Google search engine)

trainings, supportive institutional mechanisms, MIS, well-informed procurement system, SOPs, guidelines and corrections/improvement systems through continuous assessments were already in place.

Moreover, lots of efforts had been undertaken in the country to strengthen the cold chain network in past, especially since 2014–2015 onwards. This was due to introduction of new vaccines necessitating the expansion of cold chain space to accommodate the same. These vaccines included Inactivated Polio Vaccine (IPV), Rota virus vaccine (RVV), and Pneumococcal Conjugate Vaccine (PCV), in particular. Further, substantial measures were taken since 2014–2015 to create institutional mechanisms to sustain and improve the system continuously. These initiatives included the following:

9.1 Technical Resource Centres: NCCVMRC and NCCRC

National Cold Chain and Vaccine management Resource Centre (NCCVMRC) at National Institute of Health and Family Welfare (NIHFW) is a hub for developing the modules for training and carrying out training for various manpower associated with handling cold chain, for example, cold chain technicians and cold chain handlers. Besides, it carries out various assessments, studies to find out the ways to continuously improve the supply chain for immunization, including cold chain. It is also the technical secretariat that anchors the initial drafting on the technical specifications of cold chain equipment in consultation with technical subgroup of experts.

National Cold Chain Resource Centre (NCCRC) is functioning at Pune, which is under Maharashtra Government and is supported under National Health Mission. It is in fore front of trainings, research, and guidance on cold chain.

9.2 MIS System—NCCMIS

A repository of all cold chain equipment at all levels, i.e. State/District/Cold Chain Point in the system, is maintained at the National Cold Chain management and Information System (NCCMIS). It also tracks the repair and maintenance of the equipment and has cold chain space calculator, besides host of other features to help manage the system efficiently.

9.3 Capacity Building

Various training programs are organized from cold chain handlers to cold chain technicians and mid-level managers like state and district immunization officers, etc. More than 30,000 cold chain handlers, handling vaccines at cold chain points, 575 cold chain technicians and 271 program managers were already trained in last 3 years before 2020.

9.4 Development of Technical Specifications and Supplies

A recognized procedure is in place at ministry for finalizing the specification of cold chain equipment. The provisions are drafted by the technical subgroup at NCCVMRC and submitted to the apex technical specification committee constituted by MoHFW, which after examining provides the approval. While developing the specification due diligence is given in ensuring reliability, durability, maintenance and warranty of cold chain equipment with corresponding incorporations in specifications. The specifications and quantity of equipment are decided based on quantitative and qualitative inputs and as per the criteria laid under WHO-PQS standards, which are a globally accepted norm. The procurement process followed is strictly in accordance with the guidelines laid down in GFR, a two-bid system, which is transparent and impartial. Since 2004–2005, ministry is the major procurer of cold chain equipment for UIP, with some coming from UNICEF as part of donor support, especially during campaigns.

9.5 Use of IT for Stock and Temperature Management, e-VIN System

A system to track vaccines called electronic vaccine intelligence network (e-VIN) including real time temperature monitoring of the refrigerators storing the vaccine was initiated by Government of India in 2013–2014 in three states of Uttar Pradesh, Bihar and Rajasthan, which was later scaled up across all States/UTs by 2019–2020. The e-system aimed at the streamlining and regularizing the vaccine flow throughout the national supply chain network while ensuring data-driven and optimized management of the supply chain. This facilitated systemized vaccine record-keeping, digitalized vaccine inventory, enhanced capacity building of cold chain handlers and real-time temperature monitoring to track health of the vaccines stored at any level of cold chain even in the remotest areas.

9.6 Augmentation of Storage Capacity

More than 28,000 new cold chain equipment were added in last 4–5 years to augment the vaccine storage capacity.

9.7 Repair and Maintenance of Cold Chain Equipment

The country has a well-established system for repair and maintenance of cold chain, which is backed by well-trained pool of 578 cold chain technicians, spare part supplies and allocation of cold chain maintenance funds sanctioned in state government's program implementation plans (PIPs) under National Health Mission (NHM).

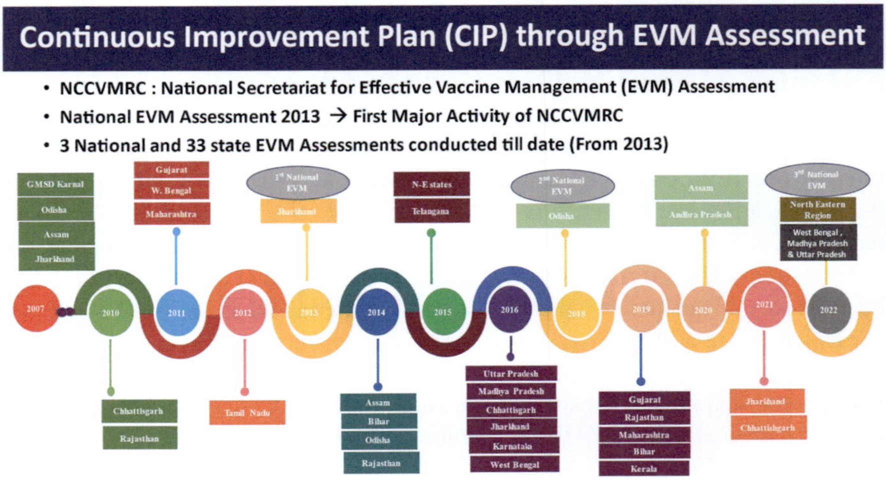

Fig. 9.4 Continuous process of improvement through EVM assessment of immunization supply chain. (Source: NCCVMRC brochure)

9.8 Assessments Conducted

To identify bottle necks in the cold chain management and with the aim of continuous improvements, ministry had initiated many assessments and studies over the years in association with UNICEF and NCCVMRC, which included national cold chain assessments, assessments of immunization supply chain including cold chain through EVM (Effective Vaccine Management) assessment. EVM assessments are continuous process and conducted periodically and provide scores against nine specified criteria, which include storage capacity of cold chain at various levels, transport, temperature monitoring, etc. Based on EVM assessment, states draft EVM improvement plans and carry out the improvements through PIP support under NHM. It ensures continuous improvements in immunization supply chain and cold chain. This also explains why there were no major hiccups during the implementation of National Covid-19 Vaccination Programme due to gaps in the immunization supply chain or cold chain network. The States were informed, knowledgeable, experienced, and largely prepared to carry out the tasks (Fig. 9.4).

9.9 Guidelines for Maintenance of Vaccine Potency

To safeguard vaccine potency, ministry had put in place numerous processes, tools, and guidelines related to cold chain system. These parameters are revised regularly as per need. These includes

- Preventive maintenance guidelines, where cold chain technician visits all allotted cold chain points once in quarter to ensure performance of equipment.

- To sustain the functional status of equipment, ministry has created a pool of spare parts at all four GMSDs. Based on the need, technicians can directly order spare parts through an online MIS system.
- To recognize heat exposure, ministry procures vaccines with vaccine vial monitor (VVM) on the label or cap.
- All the ice-lined-refrigerators (ILRs), storing vaccines, in the system have the hold over time of more than 22 h, thus ensuring uninterrupted recommended storage temperature in the event of electricity failure.
- In case of long duration power failure, a well-defined contingency exists for cold chain personnel to transfer the vaccines from electrical equipment to cold boxes where vaccines can be stored safely for more than 72 h even in the absence of electricity.
- Funds for cold chain maintenance are allotted to states through state government's program implementation plan (PIP) under NHM.
- All existing equipment in cold chain network are furnished with an inbuilt thermostat which ensures that temperature excursions beyond recommended range do not take place.
- Cold chain handlers are well trained, and cold chain points are provided with job aids to condition the ice packs before packing the vaccine carriers to prevent freezing during transportation of the vaccine to the session sites.
- There are several alert systems to monitor the maintenance of equipment.

Ministry of Health and Family Welfare has taken substantial steps over the decade to institute these practices and processes nationwide. Appropriate modifications have been carried out according to the need of the system. Through cold chain network existing up to subdistrict level, vaccines are supplied under recommended temperature up to village levels for ANMs to conduct outreach sessions.

From the above narration, it could be safely argued that the faith reposed by the policy makers to implement world's largest Covid-19 vaccination campaign through an already existing system created for UIP was not without the sound basis. Country not only had the knowledge and experience but also had a mature system, which could deliver.

For National Covid-19 Vaccination Programme, the needed cold chain storage space and equipment was calculated for identification of gaps, and this crisis was converted into an opportunity to strengthen the cold chain system further. The following steps were involved in calculation of additional cold chain space as well as additional cold chain equipment:

1. Determine the current cold chain space needed for existing Universal Immunization Programme (UIP) vaccines.
2. Calculate the additional cold chain space required for the Covid-19 vaccine.
3. Calculate the net additional cold chain space needed for both UIP and Covid-19 vaccines by subtracting the available cold chain space from the total required space (sum of current UIP and Covid-19 vaccine space requirements, i.e. CC space required for current UIP + CC space required for Covid-19 vaccine)—

(available CC space). The available cold chain space at each level can be obtained from the National Cold Chain and Vaccine Management Information System (NCCMIS).

4. Additional cold chain equipment requirement = Net additional CC space required/unit storage volume of respective CCE (rounded up to the next higher number). Covid-19 vaccines used in India Covishield, Covaxin and Corbevax required storage temperature between 2 and 8 °C. Therefore, WICs were required at primary stores and ILRs for subdistrict-level stores. Under UIP in India, ILRs are usually ILR (Large) that is 200 l and ILR (small) that is 75 l.

Thus, if the available cold chain space in terms of ml/cc/litres, volume of each dose of vaccines including UIP vaccines and Covid-19 vaccines, target children for UIP with duration of storage, daily/monthly target for Covid-19 vaccination and available doses for storage are known, it is possible to calculate the cold chain space requirements, which can then be easily converted to number of cold chain equipment. NCCVMRC at NIHFW developed the vaccine space calculator after feeding the various parameters as noted above in the tool.

While volumes for vaccines already used in UIP and stored in cold chain were already known (Table 9.1), the probable volumes of the Covid-19 vaccines, Covishield and Covaxin were obtained from the manufacturers much before these vaccines were made available for the program. The volume of single dose of Covishield (10 dose vial) was 2.1 ml, and volume of single dose of Covaxin (10 dose vial) was 1.7 ml.

UIP vaccines were delivered at fixed intervals to the states as per the target children to be covered (derived from projected population of the year concerned), and the maximum stocks, which are kept at state/regional/district vaccine stores, are for 2.75 months, and at subdistrict/block level store, the value is 1.5 months and

Table 9.1 Volume of UIP vaccine per dose and target doses per child

For WIC and ILR		
Vaccine	Vol per dose (ml)	No. of doses per target
BCG	2.6	1
Hep-B	4.4	1
b-OPV	0.9	5
Pentavalent	3	3
IPV	0.07	2
RVV	3	3
PCV	3.6	3
MR	2.6	2
JE	4.2	2
DPT	1.8	2
TT	3.9	3.5
HPV	15	2
JE	3.4	2
MCV	4	2

Source: MoHFW

corresponding minimum stock value is 1.5 months and 0.5 months, respectively. For computing the stocking requirements or cold chain space requirements of Covid-19 vaccine, the target was available as per the prioritization of the population groups in phases, and it was assumed that the whole supplies would be available at one go for transportation and storage. The volume of Covishield was taken for calculation as its volume was more than Covaxin.

The projection of cold chain space requirements was made for primary level (state and regional stores), district level and subdistrict level stores. The calculations revealed that even if the supplies of 30 million doses are given in one go, available cold chain space would not only be sufficient to accommodate both UIP and Covid-19 vaccines, but sufficient additional space would also be available to accommodate extra Covid-19 vaccine doses.

These findings were appraised by subgroup, and the technical division was asked to project the cold chain space for 300 million Covid-19 doses and plans to fill up the gaps. The estimations revealed that additional WICs and ILRs would be required to store the number of vaccines. Smaller States/UTs were found sufficient; however, the larger states of Uttar Pradesh, Bihar, Rajasthan and Madhya Pradesh were showing some gaps. Ministry had already initiated the process of procurement for expansion of cold chain and phasing out of old cold chain equipment due to expiry of useful shelf life. This procurement process for cold chain equipment was expedited, and supplies were expected to start from January 2021 till mid-2021. Similarly, UNICEF got donor support as well as GAVI support for supply of electrical as well as non-electrical cold chain equipment (cold boxes and vaccine carriers), and it placed the orders simultaneously and equipment started coming from January 2021. On the initiative of Ministry of Corporate Affairs, corporate social responsibility funds were also mobilized from PSUs for procurement of additional cold chain equipment. With these procurement-related initiatives and through close monitoring by subgroup, country's cold chain inventory saw the addition of more than 12,500 ILRs, more than 5500 DFs and around 60 WICs and 100 WIFs, which translates to more than 40 million Covid-19 vaccine doses space in ILRs alone.

Though the technical division and senior officers in the ministry were aware that Covid-19 vaccine supply would be in limited quantities to begin with, it was also known that it would improve rapidly, and therefore, there should not be any complacency. Till June 2021, by the time all procurement orders were supplied, the subgroup continuously monitored the progress on regular basis and ensured that every part of the country has sufficient cold chain space to store required quantities of Covid-19 vaccine.

Finally, it was very well understood and internalized that it is the interplay between personnel, practices and equipment under cold chain network, which is predictor of success or failure. The program had trained manpower well versed with the operations of the immunization supply chain, established practices of regular trainings, regular monitoring and assessments, regular upgradation of technical specifications of equipment and augmentation of the capacity, digital MIS and electronic tracking of stocks along with real-time temperature monitoring and large number of functional equipment backed by repair and up keep mechanisms and protocols and all of these backed by strong Institutional mechanisms. In the end, it would be apt to quote that—"*Bravery helps build resilience as challenges are overcome.*"

9.10 Conclusion

In conclusion, India's successful National Covid-19 Vaccination Programme demonstrated the power of meticulous planning, a robust cold chain infrastructure and effective management. The country's experience in running the Universal Immunization Programme (UIP) since 1978 provided a strong foundation, with an established cold chain network and a well-trained workforce. However, the scale of the Covid-19 vaccination campaign required careful assessment and augmentation of existing resources.

The government took proactive steps to evaluate cold chain capacity and potential gaps, converting crisis into an opportunity for strengthening the system. Through strategic planning, the nation ensured that available cold chain space was not only sufficient for UIP vaccines but also for Covid-19 vaccines. Procurement efforts, corporate social responsibility funding and UNICEF support bolstered the cold chain infrastructure, adding thousands of vital pieces of equipment.

This comprehensive approach, combining personnel expertise, established practices and equipment reliability (Fig. 9.5), was the key to success in executing the world's largest Covid-19 vaccination drive. India's experience underscores the importance of a well-functioning immunization supply chain and serves as a testament to the nation's resilience in the face of unprecedented challenges.

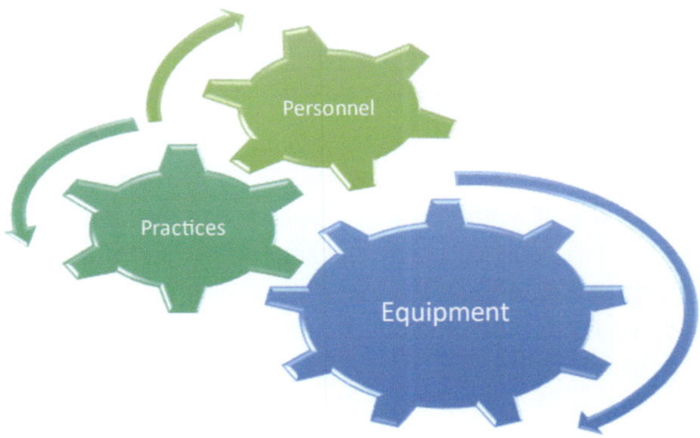

Fig. 9.5 Immunization supply chain. (Source: Open-domain/Google search engine)

Management of Syringe Supplies During the National Covid-19 Vaccination Program

10

Mahesh Kumar Aggarwal

Abstract

The syringes are essential part of logistics required to administer the vaccines under UIP as well as for Covid-19 vaccination. In UIP, three types of syringes were being used, namely, 0.1 and 0.5 ml auto-disable syringes (AD syringes) for administration of the vaccine and 5 ml disposable syringes for reconstitution of those vaccines with diluents, which are supplied in freeze-dried, powdered form. As the dose of the available Covid-19 vaccines was 0.5 ml, 0.5 ml AD syringes were used to administer the Covid-19 vaccine. The syringes were used from the stocks available for administering the UIP vaccines initially. However, the demand forecasting for the syringe requirement was done combining the demand of both UIP and Covid-19 vaccines using an Excel-based tool, named A to Z sheet. There was finite domestic manufacturing capacity of 0.5 ml AD syringes in the country and with spiraling demand for syringes due to the rapidly increasing availability of Covid-19 vaccines and improving implementation structures at ground across the country, we were staring at the disruption of the vaccination drive. A major policy decision to waive of the requirement to provide 0.5 ml AD syringes only for vaccination program and permit and procure disposable syringes of the denominations from 0.5 to 3 ml for use in Covid-19 vaccination program was taken. The daily virtual meetings with syringe manufacturers to keep tab on supplies, tapping UNICEF to procure syringes from other countries, partial export ban for 0.5 ml AD syringes, and close monitoring of the syringes supply chain up to the district level and sometimes up to the vaccination points through e VIN and daily virtual meetings with concerned state officials ensured the success for the program.

M. K. Aggarwal (✉)
Formerly at Ministry of Health & Family Welfare, Government of India,
New Delhi, India

M. Agnani et al. (eds.), *India's Covid-19 Vaccine Drive*,
https://doi.org/10.1007/978-981-95-8138-2_10

Keywords

Auto-disable syringes · Disposable syringes · A to Z sheet · e VIN · UIP · Covid-19 vaccines

Nothing is impossible. The word itself says "I'm possible!" (Audrey Hepburn)

This turned out to be the guiding "Mantra" for Team India when the country achieved the impossible looking feat of administering more than two billion doses of Covid-19 vaccine to its population in a short time span of 2 years.

In the last chapter, adequacy, augmentation, and management of cold chain for Covid-19 vaccination is described. However, there were other important logistics-related challenges which also needed attention. One such important and critical requirement was related to ensuring availability of adequate number of suitable syringes for administration of Covid-19 vaccine.

The syringes are used not only to administer the vaccines but also for medicines and drugs which are required to be administered either by intravenous or intramuscular or subcutaneous routes.

Under Universal Immunization Program, the country uses auto-disable syringes (0.1 and 0.5 ml AD syringes) for administration of injectable vaccines to neonates, infants, children, and mothers, as per National Immunization Schedule (NIS).

The auto-disable syringes are used for the administration of the appropriate vaccines, and the disposable syringes are used for reconstitution of vaccines where needed. The 0.1 ml AD syringe is used for intradermal injections. BCG vaccine and fractional dose of Inactivated Polio Vaccine (IPV) are administered through 0.1 ml AD syringe, while 0.5 ml AD syringe is used for the other injectable vaccines.

It is pertinent to mention that Covid-19 vaccines which were expected to be available in India at the earliest were Covishield and Covaxin, both having the dose of 0.5 ml and both needing administration via intramuscular route. Thus, it was imperative that the country should have plan to assess and provide required quantities of specified syringes as per available Covid-19 vaccine doses along with ensuring adequate quantities for UIP.

Well before the launch of National Covid-19 Vaccination Program in mid-January 2021, advisories were issued to the states and the Government Medical Store Depots (GMSDs) and multiple virtual review meetings were conducted by the immunization division of MoHFW, GoI, advising them to make adequate preparations to handle the high volume of the stocks of syringes including making arrangements of storing spaces, transportation mechanism, and capacity building of human resources.

Before embarking further on the assessment and availability of syringes for the program, an understanding of the procurement mechanism of the syringes for UIP is important. Immunization Division estimates the requirement of syringes based on doses of vaccines required to be administered in a year along with making calculations for minimal wastage factor and buffer needed to take care of intensified immunization drives and outbreak response campaigns.

After adding all the requirements, the indent is placed to the procurement division of the ministry along with the specifications of the syringes. After the procurement, syringes of various denominations are directly supplied to the states by the syringe manufacturers at regular intervals, as per the supply schedules given by the program division. Some amount of buffer stock and stocks for north-eastern states and smaller UTs is maintained at four GMSDs located in all four zones of the country, i.e., GMSD Chennai (south), GMSD Kolkata (east), GMSD Mumbai (west), and GMSD Karnal (north).

This system is complemented by an additional system of procurement through "Central Medical Services Society" (CMSS), an autonomous body, established as a central procurement agency with the objective of streamlining drug procurement and distribution system of Department of Health & Family Welfare, Government of India.

During the Covid-19 pandemic, the procurement of syringes was done by both agencies, i.e., ministry's procurement wing, which was given responsibility of ensuring supplies of the syringes for which orders were already placed in the past, while the CMSS, was assigned the responsibility to take over the procurement of syringes for National Covid-19 Vaccination Program.

This background is essential to understand and interpret the intricacies involved in assessment, planning, monitoring, and mid time corrections in the procurement and supplies of the syringes to the states and UTs, for the world's largest Covid-19 vaccination campaign.

NEGVAC in its very first meeting while taking decisions regarding prioritization of the population groups for Covid-19 vaccination, advised for careful assessment of logistics-related requirements of vaccination. Subgroup, II under the chairpersonship of the Secretary Department of Drugs and Pharmaceuticals, was tasked to monitor the availability of syringes for National Covid-19 Vaccination Program.

For Covid-19 vaccination, the program initially adopted the same strategy for providing the syringes, as was being practiced for UIP, i.e., the bundling of the vaccines and syringes together while supplying. Figure 10.1 provides the distribution network for the syringes used in national Covid-19 vaccination program.

However, the Covid-19 vaccination campaign was continuously evolving and was going through a very dynamic process of phase wise addition of newer cohort for vaccination, introduction of precaution dose, involvement of private sector, etc., all of which had direct implication on the syringes requirements. Hence, based on the dynamics of vaccination policy, the syringe requirements were also continuously changing, which needed prompt actions in forecasting and initiating the procurement process of required quantities of syringes.

Based on the idea of Additional Secretary In-charge of the National Covid-19 Vaccination Program, an "A to Z" Excel sheet–based tool was developed for day-to-day tracking of the syringe availability and requirement status. As the name suggests, it had columns starting from A to Z to depict the month-wise projection of syringes requirements and expected supply from different suppliers within that month to assess the overall stock status and to take strategic actions in advance.

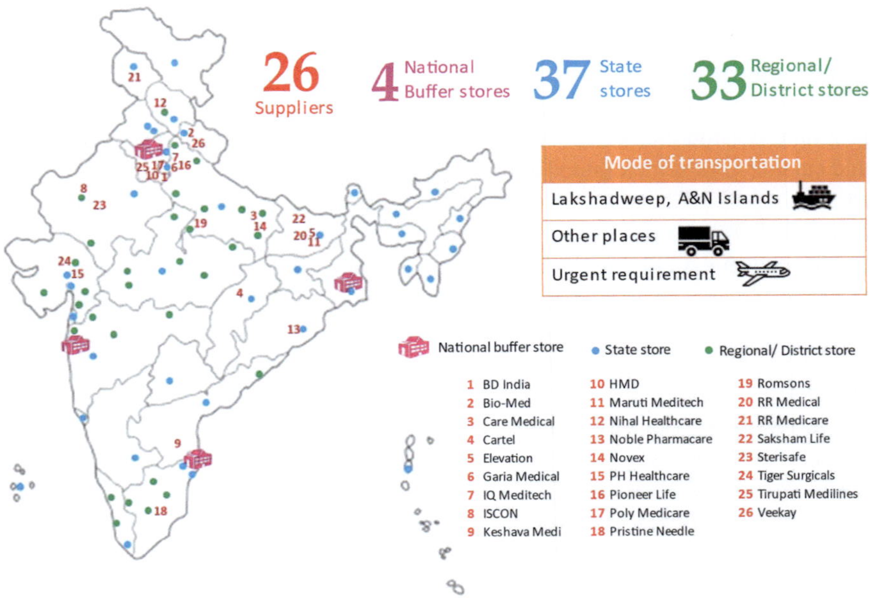

Fig. 10.1 Distribution network. (*Source*: Ministry of Health & Family Welfare)

Figure 10.2 highlights the "A to Z Sheet" for reference. In extreme left column of the sheet, the months are given and column A depicts anticipated vaccination achievements of UIP and requirement of syringes for Covid-19 vaccination program; column B to U depict various sources of supplies in that particular month; column V depicts opening balance, which comes from the last column, i.e.; Z, column W shows total supplies received during the month, i.e., sum of column B to U; column X depicts total available stock during the month, i.e., sum of column V and W; column Y depicts the syringes requirements which is the sum of column A1, A2, and A3 plus 2% vaccine wastage; and last column Z was closing balance, i.e., column X minus column Y.

This sheet became a reference and provided insights into availability versus requirements on constant basis and helped in monitoring the status of supplies from the syringe manufacturers. The actual numbers and names of the suppliers are not given in the figure to protect the commercial interests of the suppliers as well as government. The requirements and supplies were accounted for both UIP and Covid-19 vaccination together.

As a standard prevalent practice, the closing and opening balance and supplies effected during a month was regularly provided by the four GMSDs to the program division. However, since state and UT governments also procure some quantities of syringes and there was a need to get real-time information related to syringes availability, virtual meetings were organized at periodic intervals, and later this requirement was included in e-VIN monitoring system (Electronic Vaccine Intelligence Network). The e-VIN was already providing real-time data of stocks of

Month	Requirement			Total supply/expected supply against orders placed																								
	UIP	COVID-19		Ministry Tolerance			CMSS Tolerance		Ministry Regular		CMSS Regular			CMSS-GeM 35.125 Cr			CMSS-GeM Tolerance			EOI of 125cr	CMSS Global Tender	Reconciliation of stock States/UTs on 26.7.20	UNICEF support	Opening Balance	Total supplies during the month	Total available stock during the month	Requirement during the month (@ 2% wastage)	Closing Balance
	Doses administered (0.5 ml category)*	Vaccine Availability* Total	Govt.	HMD	ISCON	Carewell	HMD	ISCON	Carewell	ISCON	Carewell	ISCON	HMD	HMD	BD	ISCON	HMD	BD	ISCON	HMD	17 suppliers							
	A1	A2	A3	B	C	D	E	F	G	H	I	J	K	L	M	N	O	P	Q	R	S	T	U	V	W = sum (B to U)	X = V +W	Y= (A1 to A3)*1.02	Z = X - Y
Dec.2020									1.25	1.54			6.00											15.36	8.79	24.15	-	24.15
Jan.2021	2.51	0.38	0.38						2.11	2.00			2.35											24.15	6.46	30.61	2.94	27.67
Feb.2021	2.45	1.05	1.05	1.53	1.045		1.500		0.85	2.34														27.67	7.26	34.93	3.58	31.35
Mar.2021	2.55	5.08	5.08	1.53	1.019		1.500																	31.35	4.05	35.40	7.79	27.61
Apr.2021	1.90	8.99	8.99	2.17			1.175				2.612			4.00										27.61	9.96	37.57	11.11	26.46
May.2021	1.71	6.10	5.88									1.57		5.00	0.304	0.297								26.46	7.17	33.63	7.74	25.89
Jun.2021	2.01	11.64	10.52								2.612			5.00										25.89	7.61	33.50	12.77	20.73
Jul.2021	2.19	13.45	12.59		1.045							0.064		5.00	2.953	0.626						3.59		20.73	13.28	34.00	15.08	18.93
1 to 25 Aug, 2021	1.41	9.62	9.18											3.26	0.550	1.080								18.93	4.895	23.82	10.80	13.02
Aug.2021 balance	2.43	6.38	6.38											1.74										13.02	1.74	14.76	8.99	5.77
Sep.2021	2.43	26.70	22.00			0.922					2.612	1.504		2.54	0.536	1.175				2.50	6.38		1.70	5.77	19.87	25.64	24.92	0.72
Oct.2021	2.43	26.70	25.00		0.115	0.922		0.80		1.885	2.612						2.50			2.50	13.04		3.70	0.72	28.07	28.80	27.98	0.82
Nov.2021	2.43	30.00	25.00					0.80		1.815		1.567					2.50			2.50	13.34		3.70	0.82	26.22	27.04	27.98	-0.94
Dec.2021	2.43	31.00	30.00			0.922		0.80			2.612						2.50		0.706	2.50	13.44		3.70	-0.94	27.18	26.24	33.08	-6.84
Jan.2022	2.43							0.80				1.567					2.50		0.706				3.70	-6.84	9.27	2.44	3.23	-0.80
Feb.2022	2.43							0.80			2612						2.50		0.706					-0.80	6.62	5.82	3.23	2.59
Mar.2022	2.43							0.80				1.567					0.77	2.17						2.59	5.31	7.90	3.23	4.66
Total upto Mar2022	36.17	177.10	162.05	5.23	3.22	2.76	4.18	4.80	4.21	9.58	15.67	7.84	8.35	26.54	4.34	3.18	13.27	2.17	2.12	10.00	46.20	3.59	16.50		193.76		204.45	

Supply completed | Delay in supply | Anticipated delay: (See end) | Inspection still not offered

* Doubtful supply of ISCON till the month of Sep 2021 are excluded

Fig. 10.2 Sample of Estimated requirement and supply matrix of 0.5 ml syringes for UIP & Covid-19 Vaccination (in crores). (*Source*: Ministry of Health & Family Welfare)

UIP vaccines and Covid-19 vaccines; however, only few states/UTs were updating information related to syringes, which was later mandated to be updated on real-time basis.

Coming back to Covid-19 vaccination, NEGVAC initially recommended to vaccinate Health Workers and Frontline Workers numbering roughly 3 crores, for which it was decided that the buffer stock of 0.5 ml syringes available with four GMSDs and with the states/UTs would be sufficient and be utilized for the same. Accordingly, A to Z Sheet was presented to the subgroup in December 2020 indicating availability of syringes for covering initially recommended eligible population with two doses.

The NEGVAC later decided for coverage of approximately, 30 crore population comprising of Health Workers, Frontline Workers, adults above 60 years of age, and adults between 45 and 60 years of age with comorbidities. Accordingly, the program division projected the requirement of 66 crores 0.5 ml AD syringes.

However, by March 2021 itself, it was realized that vaccine availability for the entire eligible population is going to improve very fast and planning for syringes will also be needed to cater the entire adult population with two doses in near future.

> I'm not going to continue knocking that old door that doesn't open for me. I'm going to create my own door and walk through that. (Ava DuVernay)

From April 1, 2021, the population group comprising of adult above age of 45 years (approximately 36 crore citizens) and later on June 21, 2021, all adults above 18 years of age became eligible for Covid-19 vaccination. The adult population was huge, comprising of 94 crore citizens. The additional requirement was calculated and projected to CMSS for procurements. Order for some quantities was placed to the existing suppliers for supplies of certain defined quantities of AD syringes under "Tolerance Clause" whereby, the supplier is obliged to supply additional 50% quantity of syringes over and above the already placed order as per the bid document conditions.

It is pertinent to mention here that there were limited manufacturers of AD syringes or RUP (Reuse Prevention) syringes in the country, and most of them had commitments for exports, mainly to UNICEF, as the latter was involved in procurement of syringes on behalf of many other countries, since India was a big source for such procurements. Knowing all these facts well, the program division of the Ministry was constantly engaged through physical and virtual meetings with suppliers, requesting them to expedite the due supplies including that of under "Tolerance Clause" and to participate in the recently tendered quantities of 0.5 ml AD syringes.

Syringe manufacturers expressed their inability due to time required for production and testing and due to commitments elsewhere. To solve this, a virtual conference was organized under the chairpersonship of Additional Secretary and in charge of Covid-19 vaccination with the existing domestic suppliers of AD syringes, requesting for the same. Despite persistent and rigorous efforts, doors for additional quantities of AD syringes were not opening, which is evident from the fact that CMSS received only a single valid bid that too of only 10% of the tendered quantity from a domestic manufacturer, after floating a global tender for projected requirement of 0.5 ml AD syringes.

As a result, after due deliberations and considering all possibilities, in addition to use of AD syringes, a decision to include disposable syringes of the dominations ranging from 0.5 to 3 ml for administration of Covid-19 vaccine was taken by the government. Also, realizing that there was hardly any possibility of getting additional supplies of 0.5 ml AD syringes, in June 2021, UNICEF was requested to provide RUP syringes/AD syringes of denominations ranging from 0.5 to 3 ml as commodity assistance under donor-supported program.

However, quantities assured by UNICEF were again far less than the required and that too were not in the time and manner of requirements. Covid-19 vaccination was likely to peak in near future and as per analysis under A to Z sheet, the stocks in August 2021 were likely to be low, and there was a possibility of stock out situation by end of September 2021. Responding to the situation, CMSS floated a new tender under International Competitive Bidding (ICB) for the required quantities including that of the new specifications. However, only domestic bidders participated, and roughly half of the bided quantity could be secured. To respond this situation, a virtual conference was organized with disposable syringe manufacturers of the country, by Secretary, Department of Drugs and Pharmaceuticals, GoI, who was also chairing subgroup on cold chain and other logistics for Covid-19 vaccination. Sixteen syringe manufacturers who participated in ICB were present during the VC. As a result, additional quantity up to the fullest capacity of the suppliers was

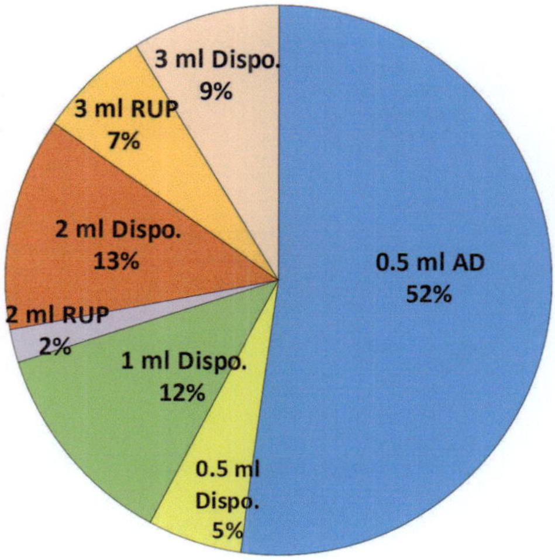

Fig. 10.3 Category-wise procurement. (*Source*: Ministry of Health & Family Welfare)

secured, and supply schedules were front loaded (Fig. 10.3). New suppliers were also identified and given supply orders.

As was expected, the demand of the syringes peaked from Mid-August to November 2021, and it was very well managed due to timely measures taken by the government. These measures are summarized as follows:

- Market assessment of the production capacity of the domestic syringe manufactures.
- Quantitative restrictions on the export of syringes for a limited period to encourage the greater participation of domestic suppliers.
- During August 2021 to December 2021, daily VCs with syringe suppliers by program division and weekly VCs by senior ministry officials to track the supply status.
- Daily VCs or telephonic conversation with concerned state officials for validating the supplies as well as to track the idle supplies in one or the other region of the state.
- Strengthening of e-VIN entry of syringes, tracking of the idle stock within the state, and arranging for intra-state and intra-district transfer as per the requirement.
- Day-wise triangulation of the supply, consumption, and balance stock data of all states and UTs to make judicious allocation of further stocks.
- Follow-up with the finance division to FastTrack of the payment to suppliers to ensure smooth production rotation cycle.
- Supply of syringes, pending test report to cut down on the supply time (i.e., relaxation was given to the suppliers to supply the syringes immediately after drawing the samples for testing with a condition that if the test results fail, the supplier is liable to take back the entire quantity at its own cost. The receiving GMSDs and State stores were also advised to keep this stock segregated and not to consume or redistribute till the QC test report was obtained).

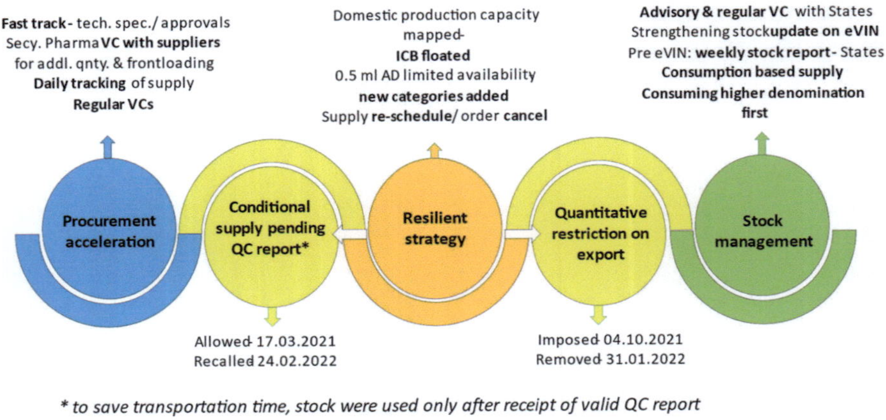

Fig. 10.4 Strategies and principles for vaccination. (*Source*: Ministry of Health & Family Welfare)

- Syringes are bulky items and hence normally shipped by road except by water to the islands like Lakshadweep and Andaman and Nicobar. However, during the peak demand time and to manage the crisis, the syringes were transported by flights to many places no/low stock situations.
- Close follow-up with the suppliers, and states receiving stores to bring down the lead time of supply to the level of bare minimum. Supplies even made on Saturdays/Sundays and other Holidays.
- Breaking the practice of supplying to the states from fixed GMSDs—As the availability and program requirement, all the GMSDs were required to supply to the stores anywhere in the country depending upon the stocks with GMSDs and consumption pattern of the states/UTs which was closely monitored on day today basis.

Figure 10.4 depicts the summary of the strategies and principles that were followed to overcome the challenge. At last, we triumphed due to the efforts put up by a team having zeal to accomplish the tasks assigned, overcome the challenges, and innovate to emerge victorious in adverse circumstances.

10.1 Conclusion

The achievement of administering over two billion Covid-19 vaccine doses in India within 2 years required meticulous planning and adaptability. Adequate syringe availability was a crucial logistical element alongside vaccine supply. The National Covid-19 Vaccination Program faced dynamic changes in vaccination policy, necessitating prompt forecasting and procurement adjustments.

To manage this, an "A to Z Sheet" was developed to track syringe availability and requirements in real time. As the adult population became eligible for vaccination, additional syringe requirements were projected and procured, even involving disposable syringes due to limited auto-disable syringe manufacturers. Despite challenges, timely measures were taken, including market assessment, export restrictions, and close collaboration with suppliers and states.

The government successfully navigated the peak demand period, emphasizing tracking, allocation, and supply chain optimization. The team's efforts and innovative approaches ultimately led to overcoming the syringe supply challenge, echoing Nelson Mandela's words, "*It always seems impossible until it is done.*"

Vaccine Safety Surveillance for Covid-19 Vaccinations

11

Mahesh Kumar Aggarwal and Deepak Polpakara

Abstract

Vaccines are administered to healthy individuals to protect against vaccine preventable diseases. Vaccines are licensed for public use after they undergo rigorous regulatory process involving pre-clinical assessment and clinical trials not only to establish immunogenicity and effectiveness but also the safety of the vaccine. However, no vaccine is entirely without risk, and adverse events may occasionally occur following vaccination. India already had an established system of vaccine safety surveillance for both UIP and non-UIP vaccines. Regular Adverse Events Following Immunization (AEFI) Surveillance Programme structures and guidelines were suitably modified and strengthened to mount AEFI Surveillance for Covid-19 vaccination drive. The advisories regarding the modifications and implementation of the revised guidelines were issued to the states. Simultaneously, large-scale capacity building efforts were undertaken to train the health managers and health care workers to recognize, manage, report and investigate the AEFIs. An entire module was created within the existing SAFE-VAC (electronic reporting system for serious and severe AEFIs) to capture minor AEFIs and enabling the reporting by vaccinators directly into Co-Win. For transparency and public trust in the Covid-19 vaccines, media was briefed on daily basis on occurrence of AEFIs and press releases were given time to time about such happenings. Causality assessments of AEFIs were expedited and reports put up on website of MoHFW. Special emphasis was given to pregnant women being administered Covid-19 vaccines. No substantial risk of the vaccines could be established in pregnant women. Under the Covid-19 vaccination program, signal

M. K. Aggarwal (✉)
Formerly at Ministry of Health & Family Welfare, Government of India, New Delhi, India

D. Polpakara
ITSU, New Delhi, India

M. Agnani et al. (eds.), *India's Covid-19 Vaccine Drive*,
https://doi.org/10.1007/978-981-95-8138-2_11

review system was strengthened to pick up any safety signal concerning Covid-19 vaccination. In addition to the existing passive AEFI Surveillance Programme, a separate study to monitor Adverse Events of Special Interest (AESI) following Covid-19 vaccines was initiated to carry out active surveillance through sentinel sites.

Keyword

AEFI surveillance programme · PSUR · ICSR · Signal · AESI · TTS · UIP · Regulatory · Clinical trials

> Misinformation or distrust of vaccines can be like a contagion that can spread as fast as Measles. (Theresa Tam)

Vaccines are administered to the healthy individuals to protect them against diseases. Therefore, it becomes imperative to ensure safety of the vaccines before they are licensed to administer to people at large. To ensure this, before licensing a vaccine, every country has defined regulatory process, developed and controlled by a Drugs Regulating Agency, which examines the data generated during vaccine development including that of vigorous pre-clinical assessment and different phases of clinical trials.

In case of Covid-19 vaccines also, a defined process was followed to authorize their use to carry out the vaccination campaign. Nonetheless, this process as per the established international norms was suitably modified without compromising the safety aspects, to make the Covid-19 vaccines available as soon as possible under "Emergency Use Authorization." India followed the same path to make Covid-19 vaccines available to its citizens at earliest, to minimize mortality and morbidity due to Covid-19 pandemic, a massive public health emergency.

Nonetheless, even after a new vaccine is licensed, its safety aspects are continuously monitored through different mechanisms by drug regulator, since this new product is now made available for administration to large number of eligible people, in contrast to the various clinical trial phases, when the vaccine is administered to limited number of volunteers. This is carried out not only to ensure that no harm is done to the vaccine recipient but also to build confidence and trust of citizens regarding vaccines as an effective weapon against vaccine preventable diseases.

In India, there are established mechanisms to conduct the post-licensure safety surveillance for the vaccines, which are as follows:

1. Periodic Safety Update Reports (PSURs) monitoring
2. Adverse Events Following Immunization (AEFI) Surveillance Programme
3. Individual Case Safety Reports (ICSRs) monitoring

Before, elaborating efforts made to monitor the safety of Covid-19 vaccines used in India, it would be pertinent to explain the basics of AEFI Surveillance in operation, as the country was already administering the vaccines against 12 vaccine-preventable disease to the children and pregnant women under Universal Immunization Program.

Although vaccines by and large are safe, no vaccine is entirely without risk, and adverse reactions may occasionally occur following immunization. It is also important to note that the benefits of vaccination far outweigh the risks related to or perceived to be, due to vaccines.

AEFI surveillance is the continuous surveillance of any adverse event that follows vaccination and may or may not be caused due to the vaccine. After vaccination, one may have minor symptoms such as pain, swelling and redness at the injection site; mild or moderate fever for a couple of days, fatigue, generalized body aches, nausea, headache, etc., which are self-limiting or can be managed with over-the-counter medications (such as paracetamol), and such symptoms do not usually extend beyond 48–72 h.

Further, Severe (or non-minor) AEFIs are those AEFIs that have a higher degree of severity (intensity) such as pain and swelling which extends beyond nearest joint, high-grade fever, minor AEFIs continuing beyond 2–3 days, intense fatigue or body aches or any other event that disrupts normal functioning and daily activities. Hospitalization is not required in these cases also and can be managed by prescribing medicines to be taken at home.

However, serious AEFIs are a subset of severe AEFIs that require hospitalization or may result in temporary or permanent disability or rarely even death. Further, if health workers or the community suspects an unusual increase in minor AEFIs, related to a certain vaccine or batch of vaccine, in a given population or over a given period of time then, clustering of such minor cases is also reported as serious AEFIs.

All AEFIs reported following vaccinations may not be caused by the vaccine. Serious and severe AEFIs are investigated, and causality assessment is conducted to know the likelihood of vaccine causing such event.

To monitor these adverse events, different kinds of AEFI surveillance are used. Passive AEFI surveillance is the most prevalent kind of surveillance. In this kind, anyone who suspects that someone has suffered an adverse event after vaccination can report such case to the nearest health facility.

After getting reported, minor AEFIs are line listed and analysed separately at the primary health centre and district levels, while serious and severe AEFIs are investigated and causality assessment is conducted of those cases having complete investigations and all supporting documents.

The aim of the AEFI surveillance system is to ultimately weigh the benefits of vaccination against the risk of morbidity and mortality due to a particular disease and also against the risk of adverse event following that vaccine. The national drug regulatory system ensures that only safe and effective vaccines are allowed for use in the country.

In India, AEFI surveillance programme is part of the Universal Immunization Programme (UIP), since late 1980s. Its focus is on vaccines that are routinely administered as part of the UIP to children and pregnant women. Nonetheless, serious and severe adverse events following other vaccines such as those given in private hospitals or are used for international travel or to protect against diseases like rabies, yellow fever, etc., are also reported, investigated and causally assessed through the existing AEFI surveillance system.

AEFI registers at every government health facility also record minor AEFIs, in addition to details of serious and severe AEFIs. The AEFI Operational Guidelines 2015 details on how the system should function, the roles and responsibilities of stakeholders at various levels, the formats to be used, the timelines for reporting and investigations, etc. Further, since 2020, a software application called SAFE-VAC (Surveillance and Action for Events following Vaccination) is being used for AEFI surveillance across the country. The SAFE-VAC currently captures serious and severe AEFIs reported by the District Immunization Officer.

The processes of AEFI surveillance within a district, state and national level are reviewed by AEFI committees at each of these levels. The AEFI committees at district and state levels are formed of clinical specialists, public health specialists/epidemiologists, immunization programme managers, representatives of drug regulators and representatives of professional associations such as IAP, IMA, etc.

The national AEFI committee is a group of experts consisting of paediatricians, medical specialists, neurologists, cardiologists, obstetricians-gynaecologists, pathologists, forensic medicine specialist, immunologists, vaccinologists, epidemiologists and public health experts and others who guide the programme and recommend changes to be made to improve the AEFI surveillance programme.

The AEFI committees are expected to review the performance of the AEFI surveillance system and to ensure that the AEFI surveillance guidelines are followed. The committee members at the district level and state level assist in case investigations, while the members of the state and national level conduct causality assessments. They also contribute in managing crisis and communicating the correct message regarding AEFIs to the media, in times of crisis.

Various activities are undertaken to ensure that the health workers and vaccinators are trained on AEFI surveillance and have knowledge about cases to be reported and process involved. Health staff are also trained to suspect and manage certain reactions that are known to occur following vaccination such as anaphylaxis and anxiety reactions. Regular trainings on AEFI surveillance are also conducted for supervisors and medical officers as part of the routine immunization trainings conducted at the district level.

The immunization partners such as the WHO, pharmacovigilance partners such as Pharmacovigilance Programme of India (PvPI) under Indian Pharmacopoeia Commission (IPC) and Central Drugs Standard Control Organization (CDSCO) are also involved in capacity building activities and sensitizing the system to increase the reporting of adverse events.

The AEFI surveillance system constantly evolves, since new vaccines are introduced and progress is made in the science of vaccine pharmacovigilance.

Now, coming back to National Covid-19 Vaccination Programme in India, one of the recommendations for introduction of the Covid-19 vaccines was to ensure that vaccine records (name of vaccine and batch number) are recorded for all vaccine recipients, so that in case of an adverse event, it is possible to know which vaccine was received by the recipient. It was known that due to limited availability, initially Covid-19 vaccines will be offered to prioritized populations consisting of the adult age group (especially the elderly). Therefore, the vaccine safety surveillance system, which was conventionally focussing on the paediatric population, required to be sensitized to collect and study AEs in the adult population. There was a need to orient medical specialists, neurologists, cardiologists, respiratory medicine specialists and obstetrician-gynaecologists to report AEFIs and include them in the AEFI committees at all levels (district, state and national levels). These new members were also needed to be trained for investigations (district level) and causality assessments (state and national levels).

It was also clear that, for world's largest vaccination campaign, special safety recommendations are given to ensure that due to programmatic errors, adverse events do not occur at the session sites.

Covid-19 vaccines even though were developed on previously well-used platforms such as inactivated vaccines, still being new, needed monitoring using active surveillance methods. Therefore, experts recommending for setting up of active Adverse Event of Special Interest (AESI) surveillance studies were not out of context.

Also, there was a need to strengthen signal detection and management systems with the objectives of rapid reviews for early recognition of AEFIs requiring intervention, timely data sharing with regulators and pharmacovigilance partners and ensuring that a clear communications strategy is in place.

At the beginning of the pandemic, knowledge and understanding about the virus's behaviour on individual and the population was evolving. Countries, research organizations and vaccine manufacturers were racing to develop vaccines against Covid-19. Keeping track of such rapidly changing environment related to vaccine development, regulatory system also needed changes to gather clinical trial data to enable expedited approvals, and simultaneously appropriate changes in the surveillance system also became a critical requirement.

By October–November 2020, it was clear that country will need to prepare for the introduction of Covid-19 vaccines which were adeno-vectored (such as AstraZeneca's Vaxzevria or Covishield as it is known in India), killed vaccines (such as Covaxin) and possibly mRNA vaccines (manufactured by Pfizer and Moderna). Some other vaccines such as Incovac, Corbevax, Sputnik and Covovax were also on horizon, but due to low probability of their immediate availability in large volumes, it was decided to initially focus on preparing the AEFI surveillance system for use of Covishield, Covaxin and mRNA vaccines.

Covid-19 vaccines were novel vaccines and were granted Emergency Use Authorization. These vaccines were to be administered to a large population in campaign mode in a short period of time. Therefore, in last quarter of 2020, based on the available information, advisory to strengthen AEFI surveillance in districts and states was issued by MoHFW on 18 November 2020. The specific points of the Advisory were:

- States/UTs to identify and partner with a medical college to establish State AEFI Technical Collaborating Centres.
- Training of specialists of state AEFI committees and state AEFI technical collaborating centres for investigation and causality assessments.
- More frequent meetings of state and district AEFI committees.
- Hiring of state AEFI consultants.
- Expanding reporting network of AEFI surveillance for adult vaccinations.
- Expanding the State and District AEFI Committees by inclusion of Medical Specialist, Cardiologist, Neurologist and Obstetrician and Gynaecologist.
- Ensuring operationalization of PHC based AEFI registers.
- Co-ordinating with Adverse Drug Reaction Monitoring Centres (AMCs).
- Ensuring involvement of drug inspectors for investigations in the districts.
- Availability of injection adrenaline in Anaphylaxis & AEFI management kits and training of vaccinators on use of Anaphylaxis kits.
- Conducting AEFI trainings and sensitization meetings.
- Preparing communication plans to address community and media concerns.
- A chapter on AEFI surveillance for the new Covid-19 vaccines were included in the Covid-19 vaccination operational guidelines, for prevention of anxiety reactions and programme errors. The procedures and protocols for AEFI surveillance in India, described in the National Adverse Event Following Immunisation (AEFI) Surveillance Operational Guidelines of 2015 were adapted for Covid-19 vaccination with following key modifications:
- Expand membership of national, state and district AEFI committees to include neurologists, cardiologists, respiratory medicine specialists, medical specialists, and obstetrician-gynaecologists.
- The Case Reporting Form (CRF) and the Case Investigation Form (CIF) were modified for Covid-19 vaccination. The Preliminary Case Investigation Form (PCIF) and Final Case Investigation Form (FCIF) were merged into the single Case Investigation Form (CIF). The timeline for filling the CIF was also made shorter than the one prescribed for routine immunization.
- Guidance was also given for ensuring better quality post-mortem by conducting videography, inclusion of panel of experts with pathologist, medical/paediatrician in the team conducting postmortems, and follow-up to get histo-pathological examination of postmortem viscera, etc.

Co-Win portal provided a unique opportunity to allow vaccinators to report AEFIs and to capture minor adverse events, which was not being done in the routine AEFI surveillance. To ensure this, an entire module was created within the existing electronic AEFI reporting tool, i.e. SAFE-VAC, which conventionally was designed to capture only serious and severe adverse events with access at the district level. By the end of December 2020, SAFE-VAC with the new module for reporting of AEFIs (including minor ones) from the vaccinator level was integrated with Co-Win.

As soon as the approvals for Covid-19 vaccines were announced, the trainings and capacity building activities were conducted in online mode. These trainings were not just confined for the immunization programme managers at the state and district levels, but it also included vaccinators for reporting of minor, serious and severe AEFIs, preventing the occurrence of anxiety reactions in clusters and initial management of suspected anaphylaxis at session sites. It is also relevant to mention that extra vaccinators (from nursing colleges, private hospitals, etc.) who were from outside of the regular system also got trained simultaneously for the same.

The members of the national, state and district AEFI committees were trained on the Covid-19 vaccination preparations and modifications in the AEFI surveillance system. The most challenging aspect was to train the new members of the state and national AEFI committees on causality assessment, which was best done through physical training as it warranted a lot of discussion and clarification. All these trainings were conducted well in advance of the launch date, i.e. 16 January 2021.

Further, for National Covid-19 Vaccination Programme, the timelines for reporting, investigation and causality assessments by the districts and states were reduced, so that the causes of AEFIs could be known as early as possible to enable timely corrective actions. Initially causality assessments took some extra time due to restricted movements and lack of necessary documents such as hospital records, postmortem reports/verbal autopsy forms, etc. Even then, between 16 January and 31 March 2021, the national causality assessment committee met six times and National AEFI committee met three times and causality assessment of 31 cases got completed and approved by the national AEFI committee. It is pertinent to mention here that all serious and severe AEFIs are investigated by the District Immunization Officer (DIO) and undergo causality assessment (which is a scientific and technical review process) by trained members of the state and national AEFI committee. Further, the approved results of causality assessment at the national level are regularly published at the MOHFW website (https://main.mohfw.gov.in/Organisation/Departments-of-Health-and-Family-Welfare/immunization/aefi-reports).

During March 2021, some European countries reported cases of thrombosis and thrombocytopaenia syndrome in those receiving vaccines based on adenovector platform. At that time, it was not clear whether there was a causal effect of the vaccine. In order to better understand this phenomenon in the Indian context, it was decided to set up a process of rapid review of reported AEFI cases based on whatever information was available and look for trends and outliers, which would require further investigations. In the first week of April 2021, an expert team was formed from National AEFI Committee to conduct the rapid review under the guidance of National AEFI Committee. It completed in-depth case review of 498 serious and severe events, of which 26 cases were reported to be potential thromboembolic events (formation of a clot in a blood vessel that might also break loose and carried by the blood stream to plug another vessel), following the administration of Covishield vaccine—with a reporting rate of 0.61 cases/million doses. There were no potential thromboembolic events reported following administration of Covaxin vaccine.

It was concluded that AEFI data in India showed that there is a very miniscule risk of thromboembolic events. The reporting rate of these events in India is around 0.61/million doses, which was much lower than the four cases/million reported by UK's regulator Medical and Health Regulatory Authority (MHRA). Germany has reported 10 events/million doses. It is important to know that thromboembolic events keep occurring in general population as background, and scientific literature suggests that this risk is almost 70% less in persons of South and Southeast Asian descent in comparison to those from European descent. The results of the rapid review were shared with the MOHFW and NEGVAC on 12 April 2021. Some cases of thrombosis and suspected cases of TTS were reported by then, but it could not be conclusively known whether this was due to the vaccine or due to some other cause such as Covid-19 infection. It was also possible that cases of TTS were not being diagnosed/suspected by clinicians and reported. Therefore, advisories were issued for health care workers and vaccine beneficiaries to identify, treat and report cases of thrombosis and thrombocytopenia syndrome (TTS) following adenovector-based Covid-19 vaccines. **It is noteworthy that Ministry of Health and Family Welfare, Government of India, shared these findings of National AEFI Committee and gist of advisory issued to the States/UTs in public domain through a press release on 17 May 2021**. In addition, the press release also contained the data on adverse events and doses of Covid-19 vaccines administered. The detailed advisory sent to the States/UTs not only contained the suspected signs and symptoms of TTS but also the guidelines about diagnostics and treatment.

Meanwhile, the frequency of meetings of the sub-committee of National AEFI Committee on causality assessments was increased from May 2021 onwards. Between 1 May and 31 December 2021, the sub-committee met 32 times (average 4 times a month). The national AEFI committee met 12 times during the same period of 8 months and approved the causality assessment results of 681 AEFI cases in this period. Further, a rapid review of 1356 AEFIs was completed and presented to NEGVAC on 24 September 2021, for information and further guidance.

By 1 January and 30 June 2022, the sub-committee of National AEFI Committee on causality assessment met 21 times (average 3 times a month), while the national AEFI committee met 7 times (at least once a month) to approve causality assessment results of 1023 cases. Over the next 6 months from 1 July to 31 December 2022, ten subcommittee meetings were held and the national AEFI committee met three times during which results of 759 cases were approved. Between 01 Jan and 30 June 2023, the national causality assessment subcommittee met three times and national AEFI committee met three times to approve causality assessment results of 214 cases. By 30 June 2023, causality assessment results of 2708 out of ~2800 serious and severe AEFI cases were approved by the national AEFI committee. The results of the causality assessments are available on the website of the Ministry of Health & Family Welfare, Government of India.

The pregnant women normally are not part of any clinical trials, due to ethical considerations and fear of affecting the unborn child. Some vaccines are recommended for pregnant women only after careful assessment of data related to adverse events recorded in pregnant women who are not known to be pregnant at the time of vaccination. There are also certain situations where the known benefits of vaccination far outweigh the unknown risk of adverse event in the mother or the child. Such a situation arose during the Covid-19 wave of April–May 2021, when it was realized that pregnant women are more at risk of adverse outcomes due to Covid-19. In July 2021, it was recommended by NTAGI that all pregnant women should receive two doses of Covid-19 vaccine as early as possible to protect against Covid-19. All cases of AEFIs in pregnant women were followed up for investigations and completion of causality assessment. A thorough causality assessment of each case was jointly conducted by a team of experts consisting of obstetricians-gynaecologists and physicians. No substantial risk could be established at the end of the causality assessment process of the reported cases.

By December 2021, when most adults in the 18 plus age group had received at least one dose, it was decided to offer vaccines to the adolescents, which were not considered to be a priority population till then. There was a fear that with the adult populations protected and with the constant mutations of the virus, it may shift to the adolescent and child age groups that were unprotected. Therefore, a decision was taken by NEGVAC to first offer vaccines to the 15–17 years age group, a majority of whom were slated to appear in the class 10 and 12 board examinations in closed rooms. Later 12–14 years age group was also included for Covid-19 vaccination in March 2022. As soon as adolescents started getting vaccinated, a dedicated team of paediatricians were meeting regularly to review the progress in investigations and the completion of case records for causality assessment. The causality assessments of almost all cases were completed within a record time of 3 months.

Then, the fear of waning of immunity after a few months (8–9 months) was considered, and again certain populations such as the elderly and frontline workers were offered a booster dose. It was considered that the booster dose should be a heterologous dose to provide an alternate channel of immunity to provide additional protection. Less than 200 AEFI cases (including minor ones) were reported following the third dose.

As per the data available as on 31 March 2023, more than 2.2 billion doses of Covid-19 vaccine were administered and around 92,000 cases of Adverse Effects Following Immunization (AEFI) including minor, serious and severe cases have been reported; however, majority of these cases were minor AEFI cases. This is only 0.0042% of all the doses administered.

In June 2022, it was observed that the reporting of minor, serious and severe AEFIs on Co-Win by vaccinators at the session sites and the district immunization officers had reduced. One possible explanation could be the understanding of the health staff that Covid-19 vaccines were generally safe, and the importance or need to report AEFIs had reduced, and they were largely focusing on improving the vaccination coverage. To overcome this, a decision was taken to allow the reporting of minor, serious and severe AEFIs by vaccine recipients in Co-Win through an online module from 30 June 2022 besides sensitizing the Health workers regarding the necessity to report each and every AEFI case. Communication regarding this was sent to the states, clarifying that the relatives/friends of the vaccine recipient or their doctors or any programme administrators who come to know of an adverse event can also report through Co-Win.

To Look for potential causal associations a Signal Review System was established as a part of AEFI Surveillance program. A vaccine safety signal is an information that indicates a potential link between a vaccine and a previously unknown or incompletely documented event. Council for International Organizations of Medical Sciences 2010 defines a signal as "Information that arises from one or multiple sources (including observations or experiments), which suggests a new, potentially causal association, or a new aspect of a known association between an intervention [e.g., administration of a vaccine] and an event or set of related events, either adverse or beneficial, that is judged to be of sufficient likelihood to justify verificatory action."

A structured approach for spontaneous reporting of AEFI is a basic element of vaccine safety monitoring. The evaluation of safety signals is part of vaccine vigilance and is essential to ensure that regulatory authorities, and immunization programmes have the most up-to-date information on benefits and risks. The benefit-risk balance of many vaccines is dynamic and may change over time or may appear to change over time, and this may impact pharmacovigilance activities.

Earlier, potential signals on specific related to vaccines were being analysed by a signal review panel set up for drugs. The need to have separate signal management system with its own signal review panel for vaccines was felt with the use of new Covid-19 vaccines. Accordingly, a signal management framework for AEFI was developed by a working group. A signal review panel (SRP), an independent body at the national level to assess information on potential signals of importance for public health, drug regulation and science from the databases for AEFIs following universal immunization programme vaccines and Covid-19 vaccines, was set up. The panel reports its findings and recommendation to the National AEFI Committee and the Ministry of Health and family welfare (MOHFW), Government of India.

In addition to the existing passive AEFI surveillance programme, a separate study to monitor Adverse Events of Special Interest (AESI) following Covid-19 vaccines was initiated to carry out active surveillance through 16 medical colleges identified as sentinel sites. Ten events are identified as AESIs and are being tracked in these 16 sites. Data collection was going on till writing of this chapter. The analysis of the data would throw more insights into the vaccine pharmacovigilance and would guide further in safety aspects of newer vaccines based on similar platforms.

As the Covid-19 pandemic ended, it was time to understand the gaps and learn from the mistakes. It was also an opportunity to strengthen the regular vaccine safety surveillance and build upon the learnings of the Covid-19 vaccination.

Immunization Division in the Ministry of Health and Family Welfare, Government of India, has established a new portal by the name U-Win for the name-based reporting and tracking of routine immunization services in the country under Universal Immunization Program, on the line of Co-Win. U-Win can be integrated with SAFE-VAC (AEFI reporting portal) to facilitate AEFI reporting and tracking at sub-district level and would also increase the reporting of Minor AEFIs. The integration of SAFE-VAC with U-Win is already under consideration of the Ministry of Health and Family Welfare, Government of India.

The changes in the Case Reporting Format (CRF) and Case Investigation Format (CIF) for the Covid-19 vaccine AEFIs were such that the same format could be used for reporting AEFIs following Covid-19 vaccinations in Co-Win and AEFIs following vaccinations under Routine Immunization under UIP in regular SAFE-VAC, making the life easy for Health Workers. The guidelines for conducting post-mortem in AEFI-related death investigations in adults and children, along with a new verbal autopsy form for adults, will be beneficial for regular AEFI surveillance. Physicians, neurologists, cardiologists, respiratory medicine specialists and obstetrician-gynaecologists will continue to be included in AEFI committees. It is part of the strategy for preparedness of the AEFI surveillance programme for future pandemics. The country is ready to set up active AEFI surveillance systems in a short period of time for any new vaccine introduced under Emergency Use Authorization (EUA) and also when vaccines are offered to new population groups (such as adults) or to vulnerable populations such as pregnant women or adolescents for the first time. The signal management processes for vaccines, which was focusing solely on Covid-19 vaccine AEFIs, are already assessing the database of AEFIs reported following regular vaccinations.

One of the gaps in the surveillance programme was the low awareness among doctors and clinicians on reporting AEFIs. A pilot project is underway to enable doctors in medical colleges to directly report AEFIs into the software. This will be complemented with regular trainings on AEFI surveillance. District Immunization Officers (DIOs) would be entrusted with the responsibility of expanding the AEFI reporting network to private and public sector hospitals. A system has been devised to expedite the causality assessment process at the national level with active participation of the state AEFI committees in the national AEFI committee meetings. It is expected that these changes will further improve the regular AEFI surveillance system in the near future.

11.1 Conclusion

Before concluding, it is pertinent to quote the developer of Inactivated Polio Vaccine, Dr Jonas Salk—"It is safe, and you can't get safer than safe" (replying when questioned on the safety of the polio vaccine he developed).

We need to establish the trust and confidence of the community in the vaccines by having a strong, transparent Vaccine Safety Surveillance System in place, which is communicative and is able to examine the safety related concerns with scientific vigour, following globally accepted norms. This was what was kept in perspective while strengthening and modifying the existing AEFI Surveillance System to take care of the needs of National Covid-19 Vaccination Program.

12 Best Practices and Innovations: Boosting Covid-19 Vaccination Uptake in Indian States and Union Territories

Palak Badhwar

Abstract

The Covid-19 pandemic necessitated an unprecedented vaccination drive across India, prompting the central government, in collaboration with states and union territories (UTs), to implement innovative strategies for maximizing vaccine uptake. These efforts spanned five key domains: awareness generation, community involvement, inclusivity, mass vaccination, and expanded access. This chapter is trying to narrate some of the most effective measures adopted by Indian States and UTs to promote and facilitate vaccination among their residents. Through these dynamic and community-driven approaches, India's community-driven approach in Covid-19 vaccination campaign not only achieved remarkable coverage but also set a precedent for future public health initiatives especially for large-scale immunization programs, emphasizing inclusivity, innovation, and grassroots engagement. By prioritizing inclusivity, innovation, and grassroots engagement, the country's efforts serve as a model for large-scale immunization programs worldwide.

Keywords

Best practices · Inclusivity · Awareness campaigns · Mass immunization · Community engagement

P. Badhwar (✉)
UNDP, New Delhi, India

M. Agnani et al. (eds.), *India's Covid-19 Vaccine Drive*,
https://doi.org/10.1007/978-981-95-8138-2_12

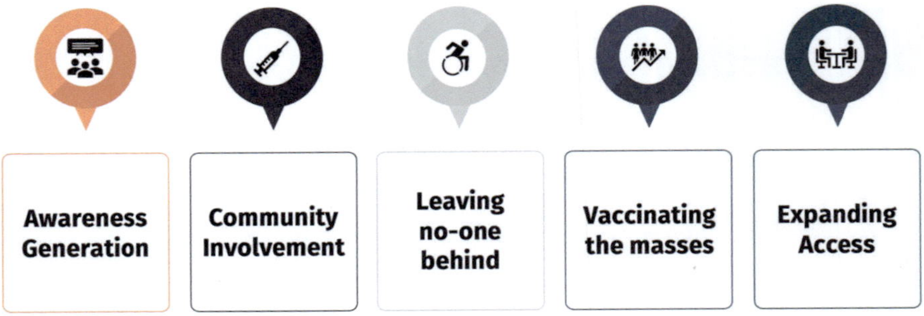

Fig. 12.1 Illustration regarding categorization of innovative measures by States/UTs

The Covid-19 pandemic presented an unprecedented challenge to nations across the globe, necessitating rapid and widespread vaccination efforts. In India, the government, along with various States and Union Territories (UTs), embarked on an extensive vaccination campaign to curb the spread of the virus. To achieve this, several innovative strategies and best practices were adopted to increase and sustain the uptake of Covid-19 vaccinations. This chapter is trying to narrate some of the most effective measures adopted by Indian states and UTs to promote and facilitate vaccination among their residents.

The central government established a robust framework for the National Covid-19 Vaccination Program with a possibility of innovations, allowing states and union territories (UTs) to tailor and execute different schemes and strategies based on their unique local challenges. For understanding purposes, these innovative measures have been categorized into five main domains as per the targeted interventions, as illustrated in Fig. 12.1.

12.1 Awareness Generation

The development of effective communication and awareness campaigns played a pivotal role in the success of the world's largest vaccination campaign. States and Union Territories (UTs) aligned with the importance of the campaign and meticulously crafted strategies that were both informative and accessible while being culturally sensitive to their respective regions. In their efforts to disseminate accurate information about vaccine safety, efficacy, and the vaccination process, these campaigns embraced the use of local languages and dialects, ensuring that the messaging resonates with the diverse populations they serve. These campaigns leveraged multiple media platforms, including television, radio, social media, and community engagement programs.

For example, in February 2021, the Maharashtra government launched a mobile exhibition, a remarkable endeavor designed to raise awareness about the Covid-19 vaccination program. This initiative saw 16 specially outfitted vans crisscrossing all 36 districts of Maharashtra, effectively becoming traveling ambassadors for vaccination awareness. The campaign extended its reach by enlisting the talents of cultural artists from the Song and Drama Division (SDD), who utilized folk performances tailored to the unique cultural nuances of each region in Maharashtra, making the message even more relatable and impactful. Such campaigns were tailored to address specific concerns and myths prevalent in different communities.

Similarly in June 2021, the Ministry of Minority Affairs launched a nationwide awareness campaign named 'Jaan Hai to Jahan Hai', with a focus on rural areas, and enlisted the support of self-help groups to ensure accurate and effective messaging. Distinguished figures from various walks of life, including religious leaders, social activists, cultural icons, educators, healthcare experts, and scientists, joined hands to deliver positive messages about vaccination through engaging street plays.

Well recognizing the fact that children could serve as essential messengers in conveying the importance of vaccine safety and promoting vaccination uptake among adults, including their parents and caregivers, in state of Himachal Pradesh, innovative methods such as poster-making competitions and the use of simple yet powerful slogans, such as *Suraksha Ke Rang Na Honge Feeke, Jab Samay Par Lagenge Do Teeke*, were employed to empower these young advocates.

In one of the schools of Chhattisgarh named as Shastipuram Madhyamik Shala, the school team curated a snakes-and-ladders game that featured vaccine-positive messages to promote vaccination and Covid-19 appropriate behavior. A student from the school mentioned that her biggest takeaway from the game was that "We learnt that getting the Covid-19 vaccine is very important to prevent getting sick and going to the hospital, that might affect our education." In Ladakh's remote Shey village, adolescents were transformed into voices of reason and assurance, addressing vaccine hesitancy within their community and neighboring areas.

Moreover, as the cohort of pregnant and lactating women was introduced subsequently for vaccination and looking to their vulnerability to the viral spread, interpersonal counselling sessions were conducted by health officials of several States/UTs to clearly share the understanding of the benefits and risks of vaccination, so as to enable them to make an informed choice.

Bihar government implemented the campaign called *Ek Adhoora, Do Se Poora* aka "Mission 2nd dose campaign" to raise awareness regarding the importance of timely administration of 2nd dose and ensure completion of primary series of vaccination of all due beneficiaries in mission mode. West Bengal harnessed the traditional art forms like street plays and folk music to raise awareness about Covid-19 vaccines among rural communities.

Local traditions and customs, such as *Khatla Baithaks* (charpai or "cot" meetings), were organized in Madhya Pradesh villages to motivate residents through public gatherings with local influencers, village leaders, and notable individuals. Additionally, the *Roko Toko Abhiyan* (stop and remind campaign) was launched to halt, remind, and motivate individuals to receive vaccinations. The state also leveraged the enthusiasm of young people by engaging "Saathiya volunteers," who are part of the "Rashtriya Kishor Swasthya Karyakram (RKSK)," in 13 districts. These volunteers used creative methods such as street performances and painted slogans on walls to educate the community about the importance of vaccination. Saathiya volunteers also accompanied healthcare workers and officials on door-to-door visits, registered people for vaccination sessions, and assisted in vaccinating senior citizens. Furthermore, the state ensured the involvement of Covid-19 volunteers through digital platforms and local initiatives to raise awareness and encourage targeted efforts for the second vaccine dose under the *Mai Hu Corona Volunteer* (I am Volunteer) campaign.

Additionally, dedicated helplines such as the national helpline (1075) and other state-specific helplines were established to provide immediate assistance to individuals seeking information about the vaccine. Trained professionals addressed queries related to vaccine safety, side effects, and the vaccination process, instilling confidence in the public.

12.2 Community Involvement

States and Union Territories (UTs) in India, duly recognizing the pivotal role played by local leaders, influencers, and community figures in dispelling myths and misinformation surrounding vaccines, made collaborative efforts by involving religious leaders, celebrities, and grassroots organizations in fostering trust and promoting widespread vaccine acceptance.

One innovative approach adopted under Social and Behavioral Change Communication (SBCC) strategies was the identification, education, and management of "community champions." This strategy proved highly effective in enhancing the acceptance of Covid-19 vaccines within various communities. Health functionaries, through consistent engagement with the community, employed trust-building measures to instill confidence in vaccines, especially among vulnerable population groups like tribal communities, transgender individuals, those residing in slums, and those working on construction sites. To achieve this, a champion-led approach was adopted, wherein members from these communities were identified and actively engaged.

For example, in Chhattisgarh, Kanchan Sendre, a member of the Third Gender Welfare Board, emerged as a prominent champion supporting outreach vaccination services within the transgender community. Sendre, now affectionately referred to as "Vaccine Didi," played a pivotal role in collaborating with the state health team, resulting in 185 members of the transgender community receiving vaccinations in her district. Similarly, in Gujarat, a remarkable initiative unfolded with the organization of 25 special vaccination camps in collaboration with local non-governmental organizations (NGOs) dedicated to empowering the transgender community. These camps were designed to cater specifically to the vaccination needs of the transgender population, underscoring the commitment to inclusivity and equitable access to vaccines.

These initiatives underscore the power of community engagement and the importance of identifying and nurturing community champions who can bridge the gap between health authorities and marginalized or underrepresented groups.

Furthermore, it is important to note that many vulnerable migratory population groups, such as truckers and laborers, faced unique challenges due to the nature of their occupations. These individuals often had to cross state or union territory borders, which required them to undergo a 14-day quarantine each time, significantly impacting their income sources. In Maharashtra, a collaborative effort was initiated with various non-governmental organizations (NGOs) and organizations like the Truckers Corporation of India Foundation (TCIF), Maratha Gramin Vikas Sanstha (MGVS), HelpAge, and the Y R Gaitonde Centre for AIDS Research and Education (YRGCARE) to enhance the mobilization of these vulnerable population groups. To effectively communicate with and reach out to these groups, a range of mid-media strategies were employed. These strategies encompassed various activities, including pictorial approach, announcements, street plays, and catchy jingles, among others. To ensure convenient access to Covid-19 vaccination services without disrupting their daily wages, several vaccination camps and drives were organized directly within the premises of migrant companies. Locations such as fuel stations, dhabas (roadside eateries), and trucking halting points like logistics hubs were chosen for these vaccination initiatives. For instance, one vaccination camp site, the Bharat Petrol Pump at Waddhamana, Nagpur, was registered on the Co-WIN platform to facilitate vaccination sessions.

These initiatives illustrate the commitment to addressing the unique challenges faced by migratory population groups and the innovative strategies employed to ensure that they have equitable access to Covid-19 vaccination services, all while safeguarding their livelihoods.

In Tripura, there exists a vibrant network of clubs in nearly every village, primarily composed of local youths. Recognizing the importance of widespread outreach, the health department forged collaborations with these community clubs to engage them in critical initiatives, particularly in the context of Covid-19 vaccination. The primary objectives were to disseminate accurate information about vaccination and dispel any myths or misconceptions associated with it. With the unwavering support of these clubs, numerous vaccination camps were successfully organized within the community. Club representatives played a pivotal role in mobilizing beneficiaries and encouraging their participation in these vaccination camps. They assessed the needs of the community through consultations at these clubs and also organized evening vaccination sessions in mobile vans. This collaborative effort yielded particularly significant results in the urban areas of West Tripura district.

Through such collaborations and innovative strategies, States and UTs in India have made significant strides in increasing vaccine acceptance and ensuring that vulnerable communities are protected against Covid-19. Importantly, these innovative strategies have also served as a model for the implementation of other health programs, showcasing the adaptability and effectiveness of community-based partnerships in addressing various public health challenges.

12.3 Leaving No-One Behind

Taking a page from the successful Intensified Mission Indradhanush, the Government of India launched door-to-door vaccination campaigns targeting specific groups, including the elderly, disabled individuals, and those facing mobility challenges.

This personalized approach not only streamlined the vaccination process but also addressed any concerns or misconceptions people might have had.

The "Har Ghar Dastak" Campaign, consisting of two rounds, was conducted to identify and vaccinate individuals who may have been missed or were due for vaccination. This involved house-to-house visits and, in parallel, a school-based vaccination campaign aimed at children aged 12–18 years. Vulnerable populations, such as the elderly, differently abled individuals, tribal communities, prison inmates, and residents of mental health institutes, received special attention in the Covid-19 vaccination drive. To ensure informed decision-making among beneficiaries, "Prachaar-toli" teams were deployed to generate awareness in identified areas before vaccination teams followed up 24 h later. Local leaders and Gram Panchayats played a crucial role in motivating beneficiaries to get vaccinated and adhere to the recommended vaccination schedules.

The utilization of local weekly markets, known as "Bazaar-Haats," served a dual purpose by creating awareness and providing vaccination services within communities. The active involvement of Civil Society Organizations (CSOs) and Non-Governmental Organizations (NGOs) contributed significantly to the dissemination of accurate information and the mobilization of beneficiaries, particularly among migratory populations. Some States adopted an innovative "Intra-State competition", at the level of District and/or Block to foster a healthy spirit of competition among districts/blocks. For instance, Manipur further enhanced this mechanism by recognizing and rewarding the best-performing district and block vaccination teams through the District Civil Surgeon.

The overarching communication strategy emphasized the principle of people's participation (Jan Bhagidari), which played a pivotal role in the remarkable success of the program. This personalized and community-driven approach not only simplified the vaccination process but also effectively addressed any doubts or misconceptions, contributing to the program's unparalleled achievements.

12.4 Vaccinating Masses

In a concerted effort to achieve broader vaccine coverage within a shorter timeframe, states across India orchestrated mass vaccination events that left a significant impact. These events, often hosted in stadiums, community centers, or other capacious venues, drew large crowds. The sheer scale and visibility of these gatherings played a pivotal role in encouraging vaccine uptake and fostering a sense of community participation.

In Haryana, an innovative initiative known as "Special Pink Sessions" was launched, exclusively conducted by women staff, aimed at vaccinating pregnant women. This approach not only ensured the vaccination of this vulnerable group but also empowered women to actively contribute to the vaccination drive.

The national capital, Delhi, introduced the "Vaccination Utsav" (Vaccination Festival), a campaign that strategically harnessed high-footfall areas such as shopping centers and metro stations to accelerate vaccination rates through special drives. This festival atmosphere created a positive and engaging environment for vaccine recipients.

The Chitrai festival in Tamil Nadu's Kallakurchi district was leveraged by state health officials to raise community awareness and administer vaccines at religious sites. Similar vaccination camps were organized at various places of worship, including temples, mosques, and gurudwaras, harnessing the spiritual connection of these locations to promote vaccination.

Madhya Pradesh initiated "Maha-Abhiyans" (mega vaccination campaigns) designed to provide a significant boost to vaccination coverage. These campaigns identified clusters of underserved populations, generated mass awareness, ensured the wider availability of vaccines, and galvanized the entire state machinery toward this concerted effort.

In Maharashtra, the "Mission Yuva Swasthya" campaign was launched, prioritizing the vaccination of students, teaching, and non-teaching staff. This campaign, conducted with the support of the technical and higher education department, organized over 2580 special Covid-19 vaccination sessions, ensuring a safer educational environment.

Haryana's Panchkula District organized several vaccination camps with a campaign focused on vaccinating adolescents and children aged 12–18 years. These camps also served the dual purpose of ensuring 100% Td vaccination among adolescents aged 16 years, thereby strengthening routine immunization efforts even amidst the pandemic. This proactive approach set an example for other States and Union Territories, illustrating the efficient utilization of resources to maximize achievements.

Furthermore, to promote the uptake of precaution doses among eligible populations, the Government of India initiated the "Covid Vaccination Amrit Mahotsava" (CVAM) from July 15, 2022, to September 30, 2022. This initiative provided free precaution doses to all eligible beneficiaries aged 18 years and above, who had completed 6 months or 26 weeks after the second dose. A camp-based strategy was employed, organizing special Covid-19 vaccination sessions at various locations, including public and private offices, schools, colleges, religious pilgrimage routes, and industrial establishments. This initiative resulted in an impressive average of 24.62 lakh doses administered per day during the CVAM period, underscoring the effectiveness of organized mass vaccination efforts.

12.5 Expanding Access

Innovative approaches to vaccination delivery have emerged, drawing inspiration from drive-through services. States like Madhya Pradesh established drive-through vaccination centers, enhancing both efficiency and the speed of vaccination administration.

Additionally, other creative vaccination centers were established to expand the reach of beneficiaries. "Near-to-home CVCs" and "Workplace CVCs" were implemented to cater to elderly individuals, especially those living alone or with limited mobility, as well as the working population, respectively. These centers brought vaccination services closer to these specific groups, making it more convenient for them to access the vaccines.

States and Union Territories have also leveraged the guidance from the Government of India for "flexi-Covid vaccination centers," enabling them to conduct vaccination sessions during evening hours. This move specifically targeted the working and service class population. For instance, Manipur deployed mobile vans with vaccination teams during the evening to vaccinate the urban service class population at key locations within urban areas. These mobile vaccination centers were strategically linked to nearby hospitals for Adverse Event Following Immunization (AEFI) management, if necessary.

Recognizing the imperative of reaching remote and underserved communities, many states and UTs introduced mobile vaccination units. These units brought vaccines directly to people's doorsteps in remote areas, tribal regions, and densely populated urban neighborhoods. This innovative approach removed transportation barriers and greatly increased convenience, ensuring equitable access to vaccinations for all, regardless of their geographic location or circumstances.

As many States/UTs have diverse geographical terrains like mountains, rivers, sea, tribal areas, snow-clad areas, etc., challenges were faced during the implementation of the vaccination program. Innovative ways were developed by local authorities to overcome these challenges. Various vaccinators along with their teams crossed rivers, climbed mountains, traversed across deserts, and all types of difficult terrains to vaccinate people every day surpassing all challenges. One such example is the village Juna Bej of District Tapi, Gujarat, which is a displaced area from Ukai Dam, and this submergence area is only accessible by boat. The people here are primarily engaged in fishing, and it is not possible for them to visit the health centers for Covid-19 vaccination. However, through the efforts of the state health officials and the district officials of Tapi, 94 people received vaccination at their residence.

Bihar introduced the "Teeka Express Model," utilizing boat-based vaccination centers to reach and vaccinate beneficiaries. This innovative approach enabled the administration of vaccine doses through 121 Teeka Express units, proving particularly valuable during emergency situations like floods.

Drones were used for transportation of vaccines in areas of North-eastern States with difficult terrains as well as flood ravaged areas, during landslides etc.

Furthermore, collaborations between government bodies and private organizations facilitated the establishment of vaccination centers in easily accessible locations such as malls, corporate offices, and residential complexes. This partnership approach expanded the reach of vaccination services.

12.6 Conclusion

These examples represent just a glimpse into the innovative strategies employed by various states and union territories in India to bolster the Covid-19 vaccination drive. Each region meticulously customized its approach to tackle specific challenges and effectively engage its distinct population. The vaccination campaign in India against Covid-19 bore witness to a spectrum of inventive practices and successful approaches undertaken by states and union territories.

From imaginative awareness campaigns that resonated with local communities to pioneering delivery methods that ensured broad accessibility, these strategies played an indispensable role in driving up vaccination rates across diverse demographic groups. By placing a strong emphasis on principles of equity, accessibility, and transparent communication, Indian states and union territories not only effectively combated the pandemic but also established a model for future vaccination initiatives.

The valuable lessons derived from these practices extend beyond the current crisis, offering a wellspring of insights and knowledge to confront health challenges that may arise in the future. In this way, the collective efforts and innovative spirit displayed during the world's largest Covid-19 vaccination campaign in India have left an enduring legacy with far-reaching implications for public health.

MIX
Papier aus verantwortungsvollen Quellen
Paper from responsible sources
FSC® C105338

If you have any concerns about our products,
you can contact us on
ProductSafety@springernature.com

In case Publisher is established outside the EU,
the EU authorized representative is:
Springer Nature Customer Service Center GmbH
Europaplatz 3, 69115 Heidelberg, Germany

Printed by Libri Plureos GmbH
in Hamburg, Germany